Come Alive!

A resource book for First School assemblies

Come Alive!

A resource book for First School assemblies

Mackenzie Coulbourne

Oliver & Boyd

For Saza, Peter and Ernest

Oliver & Boyd
Robert Stevenson House
1–3 Baxter's Place
Leith Walk
Edinburgh EH1 3BB

A Division of Longman Group Ltd

© Oliver & Boyd 1984

British Library Cataloguing in Publication Data

Coulbourne, Mackenzie
　Come Alive!
　1. Children's stories
　2. Children's poetry
　3. Recitations
　I. Title
　377'.1　　PN43045.S4

　ISBN 0 05 003635 1

Set in 11 pt Linotron Plantin
Printed in Great Britain
by Butler & Tanner Ltd, Frome and London

Contents

Summer term assembly themes

Class assembly themes

Introduction to class assemblies

General introduction

The purpose of this resource book is to assist those who are planning assemblies for children in First Schools. In no way is it intended as a textbook showing 'how to do it'. Rather, the author offers a selection of stories, poems, and ideas on hymns and prayer for twenty assemblies each term; plus a final section, with its own introduction, of material for twenty class assemblies. There is a deliberate mix of religious and non-religious themes.

The themes, as set out in the Contents list, are chosen to include appropriate seasonal features, annual events and festivals which are common to most of us. Running parallel with these, the selected themes reflect the development of children. The autumn term assemblies highlight the 'young child, the family and home'; in the spring term the themes develop the concept of 'the child at school with an awareness of the local community'; and the summer term is influenced by the 'child's widening world'. The index on page 211 gives a starting point for choosing a suitable theme and collecting the necessary material.

Story and/or poem
The reading of a suitable story, or sometimes a poem, is the main item in the first sixty assemblies. Such a reading illustrates the day's theme and stimulates the children's thoughts. Some of the tales in this selection are from the author's own experience, others are adapted from familiar literature or topical stories in newspapers and magazines. All sources are given in the acknowledgments on page 214, as are the sources of hymns and prayers not written by the author. Bible quotations are, with very few exceptions, from the *Good News Bible*.

Hymns
The first lines of suggested hymns are given, but teachers or children may prefer to choose their own.

Prayer
A prayer has been included to express briefly the thought developed in each assembly, but again a prayer familiar to the school could be chosen.

As a teacher and headteacher the author became increasingly aware of the factors which add to the challenge of leading and planning assemblies. All teachers are conscious of legal and professional obligations and a responsibility to the children and their parents, while being aware of differing religious and moral standpoints. There are further challenges invoked by an increasingly complex multi-cultural, multi-racial society, not to mention the pressure of time in a busy school day. Such diverse factors are not always easy to reconcile and a successful balance will inevitably vary within each school. This book, therefore, offers a carefully thought out selection of material from which teachers may draw, on a daily or an occasional basis, and adapt to the special needs of their schools.

1 A new school year

It's good to be starting another school year. Everything is fresh and new — yourselves, your classroom and your teachers — and you may have new clothes, books and pencils. It's a good chance to make new friends and to learn new things. That's why we welcome the beginning of a school year.

This poem to start the term is called *Day*.

> 'I am busy,' said the sea.
> 'I am busy. Think of me,
> Making continents to be.
> I am busy,' said the sea.
>
> 'I am busy,' said the rain.
> 'When I fall, it's not in vain;
> Wait and you will see the grain.
> I am busy,' said the rain.
>
> 'I am busy,' said the air.
> 'Blowing here and blowing there,
> Up and down and everywhere.
> I am busy,' said the air.
>
> 'I am busy,' said the sun.
> 'All my planets, every one,
> Know my work is never done.
> I am busy,' said the sun.

Sir Cecil Spring-Rice

We could add another verse, especially for use in school today, like this:

> 'We are busy,' said the teacher.
> 'Boys and girls — another term,
> Lots of special things to learn,
> Let's give ourselves a cheerful face
> And make our school a happy place.
> We are busy,' said the teacher.

A long time ago St Richard of Chichester wrote this verse:

Day by day,
Dear Lord, of thee three things I pray:
To see thee more clearly,
Love thee more dearly,
Follow thee more nearly,
Day by day.

Hymns: *1* Morning has broken, like the first morning
2 Glad that I live am I

Prayer: Dear Father God,
We thank you for all our blessings,
For our strong and healthy bodies,
For our families and friends,
For our school, and all the people we meet here;
Please help us to do our very best each day.
Amen

2   Birthdays

When Alesandro Malerba, an Italian boy, woke up on his sixth birthday, his father gave him an enormous parcel. It didn't seem very heavy, but it was nearly one metre wide and one metre tall. Alesandro tore away the wrapping paper and string. The box inside said 'Space Hopper' and it held a very big ball with hand-holds on the top. Soon he learned how to sit on it and bounce along. In no time he became very clever and quick with it.

One day Alesandro and his mother went for a walk along the banks of the River Brenta, near their home. Really it was his mother who went for a walk. Alesandro went for a bounce! He could straddle his Space Hopper and move faster than his mother could walk. Mrs Malerba was quite happy to walk behind him, but then she dropped her handbag. When she bent to pick it up she slipped on the wet grass and tumbled into the river.

Alesandro heard his mother shout with fright and he turned round to see her spluttering in the water. He looked around, but there was no one to help and no boats on the river. Without stopping, Alesandro gripped the ball tightly and bounced straight into the water, and a few seconds later he reached his mother, who was able to grab one of the ball's hand-holds. For nearly half a mile the two were swept along the river, clinging to the ball, until a policeman saw them and rowed out to their rescue.

When they were safe and dry at home, Alesandro said, 'I knew my mum couldn't swim, but my ball floats so I bounced it into the water.'

The policeman said, 'Without Alesandro and his bouncing ball I think his mother would have drowned.'

Alesandro's father agreed, 'He is a brave boy and I'm proud of him. I never thought his birthday present would bring such an adventure.'

Hymns: *1* All things bright and beautiful
2 I'm very glad of God

Prayer: For our birthdays God we thank you,
For health and strength,
For families and friends,
For work and play,
And all the good things we enjoy,
We thank you God.
Amen

Poem: *Tomorrow, today and yesterday*
It's my birthday tomorrow, you know;
  I feel I can hardly wait!
Although I'm seven years old today,
  Tomorrow I shall be eight.

It's my birthday today, you know;
  My cards and presents were great.
I'm having a party at four o'clock,
  My friends will never be late.

My birthday was yesterday, you know,
  And now my age is eight.
Won't it be lovely when I am nine,
  But now there's a year to wait!

Song: We wish you many happy returns of the day,
We hope you may be healthy and strong all the way;
Strong to do right, slow to do wrong,
And thoughtful for others, all the day long.
                    P. Dearmer

The story of Alesandro Malerba was reported in *The Sunday Express* (9.12.79) by John Kerr, Genoa. (The River Brenta is near Trento in northern Italy.)

3 Playtime

'Boys and girls come out to play ...' an old rhyme says. Today's children love to play! But then, children always have.

Some of your great-grandmothers and great-grandfathers played with iron hoops when they were young. Or perhaps they played diabolo — a game where a top was thrown into the air and caught on a string between two sticks. These kinds of toy could be quite dangerous, as you can imagine.

Your grandmothers and grandfathers had wooden hoops and tops, skipping ropes, and rubber balls. Sometimes they took a pack of cigarette cards to school, and at playtime they would take turns with a friend to throw one on to the ground. When someone threw a card on top of another, that child could pick up all the cards. The lucky ones went home with a pack much bigger than the one they had brought!

These days most toys are made of plastic, but your games are often the same as those your grandparents played.

Some children like singing games, others love running games, like chase and catch. What do you call the 'chase and touch' game? It could be 'he', 'tag', or 'tick', or perhaps you use another name.

Do you like playing together in a group, or just with your special friend, or do you like to play on your own sometimes? Do you have a climbing frame, tree trunks to clamber along, or painted lines on the playground for hopscotch? Is your school lucky enough to have a field where you can practise head-over-heels, cartwheels or handstands — when the grass is dry?

At home, of course, playtime is different, with special friends and maybe brothers or sisters, and your own toys and games. Then at bedtime you can lie and daydream just one more adventure, like the child in this poem.

The island
If I had a ship,
I'd sail my ship,
I'd sail my ship
Through Eastern seas;
Down to a beach where the slow waves thunder —
The green curls over and the white falls under —
Boom! Boom! Boom!
On the sun-bright sand.
Then I'd leave my ship and I'd land,

And climb the steep white sand,
And climb to the trees,
The six dark trees,
The coco-nut trees on the cliff's green crown —
Hands and knees
To the coco-nut trees,
Face to the cliff as the stones patter down,
Up, up, up, staggering, stumbling,
Round the corner where the rock is crumbling,
Round this shoulder,
Over this boulder,
Up to the top where the six trees stand. . .

And there would I rest, and lie,
My chin in my hands, and gaze
At the dazzle of sand below,
And the green waves curling slow,
And the grey-blue distant haze
Where the sea goes up to the sky. . .

And I'd say to myself as I looked so lazily down at the sea:
'There's nobody else in the world, and the world was made for me.'

A. A. Milne

Hymns: *1* At half-past three we go home to tea
2 Who built the ark?

Prayer: We remember how good it is to have time to play,
We remember the times we have fun with friends
and sisters and brothers,
For all our happy times, we thank you, Father God.
Amen

4 Jonathan shares an adventure

Jonathan could do all kinds of things — and do them very well. By the time he was eight, he could read almost anything. At Christmas he acted in the school play, and everyone knew how well he wrote stories and painted pictures. He was even learning to play the piano and the flute. But if his mother ever suggested going swimming, or trying the assault course in the Country Park — then that was different; he couldn't do it.

It wasn't that Jonathan thought these things were no fun, but he was frightened that the exercise and excitement would bring on one of his asthma attacks. Then it was hard for him to breathe, and he wheezed painfully. So Jonathan, like many people who suffer from asthma, didn't want to try such things.

Then he was lucky enough to go to a hospital where the physiotherapist, Mrs Bell, wanted to help children like Jonathan. Mrs Bell had a great idea. She knew that if children had proper medicine, and learned how to take exercise, they could also learn how to get over an asthma attack if they did have one. She made very careful plans, and prepared a really exciting week for ten children, including Jonathan. Doctors, nurses, mothers, fathers and teachers were all invited to help. Mrs Bell wanted everyone to see how well the children could learn to look after themselves.

What an adventure they had! Most mornings began with swimming, then exercise or a game before lunch. Each afternoon they went on a visit. They explored famous country houses, enjoyed an adventure playground by the sea, visited a yacht club, were taken out in a boat, went fishing, and saw a circus.

They even went to the Country Park where the assault course was. Jonathan had been scared of it, but he was persuaded to try the course and to his great surprise he found he could do it. So he tried again — and then again, shouting with excitement at his success.

All the children surprised themselves. They took the medicine the doctors gave them and tried everything that Mrs Bell prepared for them. When any of them began to feel ill, they were shown how to get over the attack as quickly as possible.

By the end of the week everyone said that it had been well worth while. The children were swimming and running better than ever before, and feeling very happy and pleased with themselves. Two months later, Mrs Bell had one last surprise for them — a visit to a big Sports Centre, to demonstrate their swimming. Three days before the trip Jonathan had to go into hospital, but at the last minute he was told that he could go with the others after all. He was so relieved!

At the Sports Centre they met David Wilkie, the swimmer, and Alan Pascoe, the runner. These famous sportsmen have both won Olympic medals. Alan explained that he had suffered from asthma since he was a baby, but he thought no one need be beaten by it.

The two athletes swam in the pool with the children, which was exciting enough. But there was one more treat for Jonathan and his friends that day. A television company had heard about their visit, and the camera crew were there. Jonathan and a girl called Sharon were chosen to tell the viewers about their adventures, and how much they had learned — thanks to Mrs Bell, the doctors, and all the others who had helped them.

Sayings: Every day in every way I'm getting better and better.
Early to bed and early to rise, makes a man healthy, wealthy and wise.

Poem: For all the strength we have
To run and leap and play,
For all our limbs so sound and strong,
We thank thee Lord, today.

Make all thy children, Lord,
Happy and strong as we,
To run and leap, and work and play,
And praise thee joyfully.

Anon.

Hymns: *1* Hands to work and feet to run
2 He gave me eyes so I could see

Prayer: We thank you God for all the good things we share. Especially we thank you for all the people who love and help us.

Amen

The Exercise and Living Tolerance Course was organised by consultant paediatrician Dr D. Hide, and physiotherapist Mrs L. Bell, of the Royal Isle of Wight County Hospital, in August 1981.

5   Hayley's helping hand

A new baby in the family is a very special event. Everyone asks if the baby is a boy or girl and if it is healthy and strong. Mothers and fathers watch carefully to make sure their child can see and hear properly, and that it learns to walk and talk at the right age. But not all babies are born perfect. A few are born with something wrong with their body or brain, and need special help as they grow up. If their handicap is very bad, these children can go to special schools to have extra teaching help and care.

This story starts with a teacher of mentally handicapped children. She stopped work and had three children of her own, and was happy that they were strong and healthy. As they grew up she told them about the children she used to teach, and the special help they needed.

Her eldest child was called Hayley. She was a kind girl, and by the time she was eight had many friends at school and in the Brownies. Her two brothers were Kerry, who was then seven, and five-year old Robin. Every week their mother took them for swimming lessons at the Leisure Centre.

One day the swimming instructor, Mr Maloney, had organised a display about Special Olympics.

'What are Special Olympics?' asked Hayley.

He explained, 'The idea of Special Olympics is to give mentally handicapped people the chance to take part in all kinds of sports. There are many famous sportsmen and women, and helpers of all ages, who want to give these people the chance to run and jump, to swim, skate or throw balls, or even to race in wheelchairs, but we need more helpers and lots of money.'

'What a good idea,' said Hayley. 'I'd like to help! I've got eighty-five pence in my money box and I'll give you that.'

Mr Maloney was surprised and pleased that she wanted to give her money to the fund. 'Would you like to come to the pool when some of the children are learning to swim?' he asked.

When the day came, Hayley and her brothers went to watch. Mr Maloney asked them if they would like to hand out the armbands and swim-rings. Hayley chatted to the children and in no time she was in the pool herself, helping them to follow their teacher's advice. Robin and Kerry encouraged the boys and girls from the edge of the pool.

Next day Hayley told her family, 'I'd like to raise money for Special Olympics. If I can get some wool I could sell knitting sets.'

Carefully she wrote a card to put in a local shop window. On the card she explained about Special Olympics and asked for any spare knitting wool. As people gave wool, Hayley and her brothers wound it into small balls. She put the wool and a pair of knitting needles onto trays that her mother had saved from the supermarket, then covered them with transparent film. The needles cost twenty-eight pence a pair, so at first Hayley didn't make much money. She decided to write to the needle factory, telling them about her idea.

'Do you think I could buy a boxful a little cheaper?' she wrote.

To her surprise she received a parcel with a letter saying, 'Dear Hayley, We are pleased to send you sixty pairs of knitting needles as a gift, to help with your work for Special Olympics.'

The children had other ideas for raising money. They decided to try to sell some of their toys. Hayley went to see the school Head to ask, 'Please may I sell our spare toys at lunch time, and give the money to the Special Olympics fund?'

He thought it was a good idea and replied, 'Why don't you see if your friends would like to do the same?'

The following day, after a very busy half-hour, the sale had raised £28!

Another of Hayley's ideas was to have concerts at home with Kerry and Robin. Their friends paid five pence each to listen to singing and recorder playing. On Hallowe'en they dressed up as ghosts and played 'trick or treat', and on Guy Fawkes night they begged for a 'Penny for the Guy', but they always showed posters about the Special Olympics fund.

A girl who was getting married gave her collection of soft toys to Hayley, who said to her mother, 'Wouldn't it be lovely if I could sell them on a stall in the market!' Her mother agreed, they managed to hire a stall and they held a very successful sale.

On Christmas Eve the Leisure Centre held its usual sponsored event — 'Swim a mile with Father Christmas' — so Hayley and Kerry joined in. It took them one and a half hours to swim the mile, but friends who sponsored their swim gave £22 to help the fund.

When Special Olympics held a Swimming Gala, the organisers asked if Hayley and her brothers could have an afternoon off school to present some medals to the winning swimmers. The medals had been bought with the money that Hayley, Kerry and Robin had worked so hard to collect. It was a wonderful way to see the results of their work. Together they had raised £200, but Hayley hopes to bring that total to £1000 one day.

Hymns: *1* Hands to work and feet to run
2 For all the strength we have

Prayer: We thank you Father God for all the blessings we enjoy. Bless all those who need your special love and care, and show us how we can help. *Amen*

Special Olympics U.K. of 57 Baker Street, London, W1, is a charity which aims to bring the opportunity of sport and active recreation to those suffering mental handicap.

6 Going through a canal lock

'There's a good place to moor up! Under those trees it will be cool at lunch time, and it's close to the lock we have to go through this afternoon.' As he said this, Arthur steered the long motor cruiser close to the grassy bank of the canal.

Ernest jumped from the bow of the boat on to the bank, and Betty leapt from the stern. Both carried mooring ropes which they secured to the bollards that stood half hidden in the long grass. They then called at the lock-keeper's house.

'Lunch-time!' the woman who answered informed them cheerily. 'The gates will be opened at one o'clock.'

Ernest replied, 'That's fine, we'll see you later.'

When they returned to the boat, Arthur and Margaret were already sitting in the cool cabin. The table was laid with an inviting spread of fresh bread and butter, salad, cheeses and lots of fruit.

The four were sharing a holiday on the canal, enjoying the peace of cruising along the quiet waters, the excitement of going through the locks, and the fun of exploring the streets and shops of nearby villages.

It was a very hot day and they were glad to rest in the shade for a while.

'One o'clock already,' Margaret reminded them. Ernest and Betty again jumped on to the bank to release the boat from its moorings, while Arthur started the engine. Gently the boat moved into the middle of the canal and entered the lock through the open gates.

The same woman greeted them again. 'My husband has been called away and I'm working the lock today.' She smiled in a friendly way as she turned the wheel to close the giant gates behind their boat. Walking to the gates at the other end of the lock, she paused to pick up a cone from beneath the fir tree that was part of her pretty garden. Perhaps she had noticed Betty looking at the tree admiringly. 'Here you are — a souvenir of your holiday, ' she said, throwing the cone to Betty.

'I was just admiring your garden. Thank you very much,' Betty replied as she caught it.

The lock-keeper's wife opened the paddles on the other gates, and as the water gushed out the boat gently dropped to the level of the next stretch of canal. Then the big gates opened, the boat glided forward and they waved goodbye.

That evening Betty gazed thoughtfully at the fir cone. They were having a good holiday, yet she wished she could wave a magic wand

and let some of their family and other friends share it with them. But their children were grown up, their grandchildren were at school, and besides, the boat couldn't possibly hold all the people she would like to invite!

Later, when they were home again, and the holiday photographs tucked in an album, the little cone lay in a wooden bowl on a shelf in the kitchen. Around Christmas time Betty noticed that the scales of the cone had opened. The seeds that lay at the base of each scale were beginning to drop out.

'I wonder if I could grow some little fir trees?' she said to Ernest. She filled a margarine tub with seed compost and dropped in the fir seeds, then added a little water before putting the tub in a warm place, inside a plastic bag.

For weeks nothing happened, then one day a few tiny spikes pushed through the surface of the soil. Betty removed the bag and put the tub into the conservatory.

'It'll be warm in here, and the shoots will catch the spring sunshine,' she thought.

It was exciting to see the tiny trees growing steadily over the next few weeks. When they were big enough, she prepared little pots full of soil, and carefully moved each plant into its own pot. Fifteen tiny fir trees now stood in a tray, growing greener and stronger as the weeks went by. When the roots began to show through the holes in the bottom of the pots, it was time to move them into bigger containers with more soil. Then they were ready to stand outside against a sunny wall in the garden.

When their family and friends came to visit, Betty and Ernest told the story of the little fir cone and asked everyone if they would like to have a tree to take home. Gradually the trees were shared out. One went to Scotland, another to Cheshire, others went to London, Hertfordshire and Hampshire. Two little trees were given to local schools.

As Betty planted one of the trees in her own garden, she remembered their canal holiday. 'Our family and friends did share the holiday with us after all,' she thought happily.

Poem:
Tall trees
With their feet in the earth
And their heads in the sky
The tall trees watch
The clouds go by.

When the dusk sends quickly
The birds to rest,
The tall trees shelter them
Safe in a nest.

Eileen Mathias

11

Hymns: *1* Over the earth is a mat of green
2 The flowers that grow in the garden

Prayer: We thank you Father God for the wonderful world we live in. We remember that as the tall fir trees grow from tiny seeds from a cone, so happy days can grow from kind thoughts and helpful hands. *Amen*

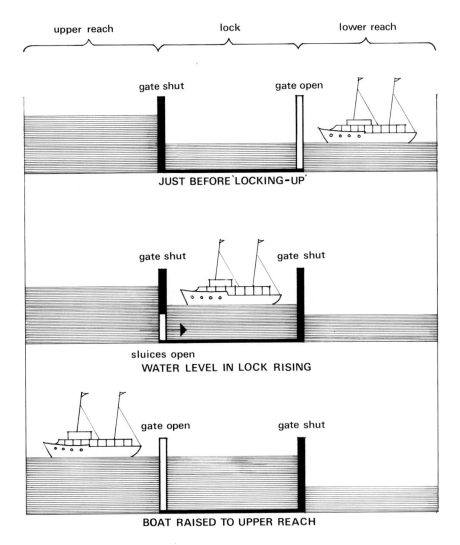

The workings of a canal lock.

Lock on the Caledonian Canal, Fort Augustus.
Photograph: Topham

7 Harriet and the matches

On a cold winter's night there's nothing like sitting beside a warm fire to make you feel cheerful and comfortable. It's fun to light a bonfire and then poke it until the sparks fly high in the sky. Sometimes on the 5th of November, the day we remember Guy Fawkes, friends gather together for a fireworks party. They build a bonfire and burn a guy, watch a fireworks display and then finish the evening with a barbecue or picnic supper.

But playing with fire can be dangerous, as you will hear in this terrible tale about a girl called Harriet, who didn't do as she was told.

Harriet and the matches
It's really almost past belief
How little Harriet came to grief.
Mamma and Dad went out one day
And left her all alone to play.

Now, on the table close at hand,
A box of matches chanced to stand;
And kind Mamma and Dad had told her,
That, if she touched them, they should scold her.
But Harriet said, 'Oh, what a pity!
For, when they burn, it is so pretty;
They snap, and burn from red to blue;
All other people light them too.'

  The pussy-cats heard this,
  And they began to hiss,
  And stretch their claws
  And raise their paws;
  'Me-ow,' they said, 'me-ow, me-o!
  You'll burn to death if you do so.'

But Harriet would not take advice,
She lit a match, it was so nice!
It crackled so, it burned so clear —
Its light shone out, why should she fear?
She jumped for joy and ran about
And was too pleased to put it out.

The pussy-cats saw this
And said, 'Oh, naughty, naughty Miss!'
And stretched their claws
And raised their paws:
'Tis very, very wrong, you know,
Me-ow, mee-o, me-ow, me-o!
You will be burnt, if you do so.'

And see! Oh! what a dreadful thing!
The fire has caught an apron-string;
Her apron burns, her arms, her hair;
She burns all over, everywhere.

Then how the pussy-cats did mew,
What else, poor pussies, could they do?
They screamed for help, 'twas all in vain.
So then they said; 'We'll scream again;
Make haste, make haste, me-ow, me-o,
She'll burn to death, we told her so.'

So she was burnt, with all her clothes,
And arms, and hands, and eyes and nose;
Till she had nothing more to lose
Except her little scarlet shoes . . .
And nothing else but these was found
Among her ashes on the ground.
        Dr Heinrich Hoffman (adapted)

Proverbs: His money burns a hole in his pocket!
The burnt child dreads the fire.
Now these are the Laws of the Jungle, and many and mighty are they;
But the head and the hoof of the Law and the haunch and the hump is OBEY.   Kipling, *First Jungle Book*

Hymns: *1* Stand up, clap hands, shout thank you Lord
2 Jesus, friend of little children

Prayer: With our hands we feel the warmth of fire,
        With our eyes we see its glow.
        Help us to listen and learn, dear God,
        Then its burning we'll never know.
                        Amen

15

8 People and everyday things

Let's think about people. Let's think about old people, young people, and those in between; black and white people, boys and girls, men and women — all so different in many ways, but so alike in others!

Here is a poem about the ways in which we are all alike, called *Everyday things*.

Millionaires, presidents — even kings
Can't get along without everyday things.

Were you president, king or millionaire,
You'd use a comb to comb your hair.

If you wished to be clean — and you would, I hope —
You'd take a bath with water and soap.

And you'd have to eat — if you wanted to eat —
Bread and vegetables, fish and meat;

While your drink for breakfast would probably be
Milk or chocolate, coffee or tea.

You'd have to wear — you could hardly refuse —
Under clothes, outer clothes, stockings and shoes.

If you wished to make a reminding note,
You'd take a pencil out of your coat;

And you couldn't sign a letter, I think,
With anything better than pen and ink.

If you wanted to read, you'd be sure to look
At newspaper, magazine, or book;

And if it happened that you were ill,
You'd down some oil or choke on a pill.

If you had a cold, I can only suppose
You'd use a handkerchief for your nose.

When you wanted to rest your weary head,
Like other folks, you'd hop into bed.

Millionaires, presidents — even kings —
Can't get along without everyday things.

Jean Ayer

Hymns: *1* Go tell it to the mountains
2 The family of man
3 For the beauty of the earth

Prayer: We remember — the help of our teachers,
the kindness of friends,
the love of our families,
and thank you God for everything.
Amen

9 The saddler's son

Who?
Who is that grumpy-looking man
Who's sitting over there?
He looks as cross as anyone can,
Uneasy in his chair.
A gloomy look, and then a frown
Furrows his worried brow.
Some problem must have got him down.
Shall I address him now?
Perhaps he's had a bitter blow,
Or made a foolish error.
I rose. He rose. I walked across,
And stood before — a mirror!
John Morrison

What a pity to look in a mirror and find a grumpy face! Let's close our eyes and think of all the lovely things we see that make us feel happy: red apples on a tree waiting to be picked ... our favourite dinner, hot and steaming, ready to be eaten ... a football match ... a favourite television programme ... buckets and spades on a sandy seaside beach ... the woods in autumn or the spring flowers in the park ... a beautiful sunset ... or the smiles on the faces of our families and friends. The list would grow longer and longer if we all added our own ideas. But what if you opened your eyes and everything was dark, and you couldn't see a thing! This is what happened to a little boy called Louis, who lived in a small stone cottage in France a long time ago.

His father was a saddler, and Louis loved to go into the workshop and watch him working on horses' saddles and harnesses. He liked the smell of the leather, the shiny knives and other tools and the boxes of nails that lined the bench. One day, when Louis was only three, there was a dreadful accident. No one really knows what happened, but he must have picked up a piece of leather and a knife and tried to copy his father. When the knife slipped Louis badly injured his eye. The sight in both eyes was affected and by the time he was five Louis was totally blind.

When he went to school it was difficult for him to learn, but he was a bright boy who listened carefully to the teacher. His father made him a board and knocked round-headed nails into it. They were close together and formed the letters of his name LOUIS BRAILLE. By feeling the nail-heads with his fingertips, Louis learned the shape of the letters. His teachers were surprised to find how quickly he learned without being able to see. They told his father how clever Louis was, and that he should go to a special school in Paris for blind children.

When he was twelve Louis left his village home and went to live in the big school in Paris. He was very sad to leave home, but soon made new friends and settled down to his lessons.

The boys were taught to read from cardboard books with big raised letters which they could feel with their fingertips. But the books were clumsy and reading took a long time.

Then the army offered the school a kind of 'Night Writing' which they used to understand messages in the dark. Soldiers on night duty used cards with dots and dashes punched in them that stood for certain sounds. Louis and his friends thought it might have been a good idea for the army, but it didn't help them very much.

However, the army's Night Writing gave Louis an idea. He began to work on a special alphabet to help his friends read more easily. He spent a long, long time trying different ways of arranging raised dots and dashes on paper. When his friends found it difficult to feel the dashes, he left them out and started his work again with dots only. At last the alphabet was finished, and it worked! Louis and his friends, who were young men by then, could read the letters quite quickly, and they learned to write the new alphabet with a special tool.

Blind people all over the world can now read books and newspapers printed in the 'Braille' alphabet. The stone cottage where Louis Braille was born is now a museum, which anyone can visit.

Hymns: *1* He gave me eyes so I could see
2 I have seen the golden sunshine

Prayer: We thank you Father God for the wonderful gift of sight. We remember the words of our hymn —

Eyes to see and ears to hear
God's good gifts to me and you;
Eyes and ears he gave to us
To help each other the whole day through.
Amen

Braille alphabet:

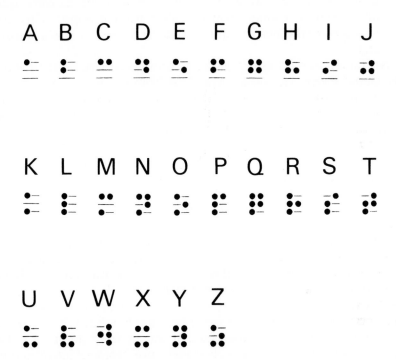

A B C D E F G H I J

K L M N O P Q R S T

U V W X Y Z

Bible story: Blind Bartimaeus healed by Jesus. *Mark* 10.46–52

10 Warning of danger

'Shouting in the playground, traffic in the street;
Television blaring, hear those noisy feet!'

These are noises that we all know well. Now listen to some quiet
sounds — a clock ticking; a whisper; a pin being dropped. This story
is about a boy who heard a quiet sound and knew it was a warning
of danger.

An Indian boy lay asleep under a cottonwood tree on the bank of
the Grand River. He was alone and far from his village. All morning
he had hunted with bow and arrows through the woods, but he had
not seen one rabbit or squirrel. At last, hot and tired, he lay down
to rest and fell asleep. The boy's name was Slow. Some day, when
he was older and had done brave deeds, his father would give him
another name. He was then twelve, and he was called Slow because
he took time to think before he acted. An Indian boy needed to think
carefully as there were many dangers.

Slow awoke with a start. Overhead he heard a tapping noise. He
looked up and saw a yellow bird sitting on a branch of the cottonwood tree; his beak was tapping sharply.

'Your noise woke me up,' Slow scolded the bird. Suddenly he
heard another sound. Something was crashing through the woods.
Out of the trees rushed a brown grizzly bear!

The frightened boy lay still, not knowing what to do. Even brave
warriors were afraid of these fierce beasts. Slow knew it was no use
fighting, his arrows were too small. It was no use running, a grizzly
could run faster than a man. It was no use jumping into the river,
a grizzly could swim. It was no use climbing the cottonwood, a
grizzly could climb trees.

'No,' Slow thought, 'it's best to lie still,' so he shut his eyes and
played dead.

On came the bear, right up to the boy, who hardly dared breathe.
The bear nosed Slow's moccasins. It sniffed his bare legs. Slow could
feel the bear's rough shaggy hair brushing his body, and hear its
huffing growls. Although he couldn't see the bear, Slow knew how
fierce it would look, with its huge paws, big yellow teeth and claws
that were as sharp as arrowheads. He felt the grizzly's hot breath on
his face.

Then, as noisily as it had come, the bear left. Slow opened one eye
and watched it go. He lay until he could no longer hear it crashing
through the woods, then he sat up.

The little yellow bird was looking at him and Slow knew that the bird had saved his life by waking him with its tapping.

'Pretty yellow bird, I will never forget you, and all my life I shall be a friend to birds because of you,' he told it.

When Slow grew up he became a brave warrior. His father named him Sitting Bull and in time he became the most famous Indian Chief that America has ever known.

Adapted from Lavere Anderson, *Sitting Bull, great Sioux Chief*

Poem: *Hiawatha's brothers*
Then the little Hiawatha,
     Learned of every bird its language,
Learned their names and all their secrets,
     How they built their nest in summer,
Where they hid themselves in winter,
     Talked with them whene'er he met them,
Called them 'Hiawatha's Chickens'.
                                    H. W. Longfellow

Hymns: *1* All things which live below the sky
2 I love God's tiny creatures

Prayer: Dear God, thank you for the sounds we love to hear; the voices of our families and friends; the sound of music; and the song of the birds. *Amen*

11 Two men and a violin

Imagine touching cold, powdery snow. Then imagine touching a hot and greasy sausage straight from the pan! Your skin can tell the difference between them. Which would you rather touch, the prickly spines of a cactus plant, or a smooth shiny apple?

This story is about two men and a violin. Eugene was a violinist who played with a small group of musicians in a London restaurant, and Mark was a young man who had always wanted to make his own violin. Eugene had promised that if Mark ever did make a violin, he would play it in the restaurant.

The only woodwork that Mark had ever done was to put up shelves in his kitchen, so he knew he would need help to make a violin. A college in London gave lessons, and he learned about the special tools and wood that he would need, and how to begin by making the ribs, or sides, of the instrument.

After a while Mark found that he was so busy with his office work that he couldn't carry on with his lessons at the college. He made up his mind that he would finish his own violin at home.

His spare bedroom became the workshop, and an old kitchen table was turned into a fine workbench. There was a lot still to learn so Mark searched until he found a book that told him all he needed to know. Whenever he saw a violin in a shop or museum he would look at it carefully, and explore its shape and patterns with his fingertips.

For a year Mark worked in his workshop whenever he could. He bought blocks of beautiful maple wood for the back, scroll and neck of the violin, fine-grained spruce for the front, and rosewood and ebony for the fittings. Gradually he collected all the tools he needed, and even made simple ones himself. His favourite tool was a tiny plane only half an inch long.

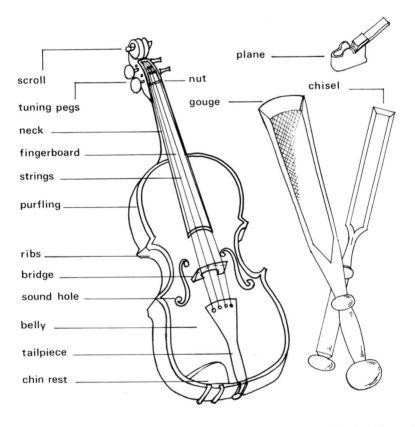

The parts of a violin.

Woodworking tools.

Gradually the violin took shape as Mark worked with his knives, chisels and planes. He learned how to use special pearl glue, and began to experiment with varnishes with exciting names like cinnabar, sandarach, gamboge and dragon's blood!

After 700 hours of work, the violin was finished. Mark was looking forward to showing it to his friend Eugene, so he took his wife and some friends to the restaurant one evening. Mark was proud to hand the violin to Eugene, who looked at it admiringly then tucked the instrument under his chin, raised his bow, and began to play a gentle gypsy lullaby. Then the music changed — like lightning Eugene's fingers and his dancing bow played a fast reel.

People in the restaurant liked to hear music as they ate, but they usually chatted with friends at the same time, seldom really listening to the music. But on this night, Mark realised that everyone had stopped talking and was listening to the music from his violin. He was so happy when Eugene played his favourite song, 'The Londonderry Air'.

Mark's fingers had made a beautiful violin, and now Eugene's fingers were playing it so well. All the hard work had been worth while!

Poem: *Finger feelings*
My mummy says clever little fingers can —
   Knock on wood,
     Be quite good;
   Flick a switch,
     Sew a stitch;
   Tickle toes,
     Pluck a rose;
   Pull on socks,
     Wind up clocks;
   Stroke the kittens,
     Knit baby's mittens;
   Prick a bubble,
     Get into trouble;
My little fingers can pick up a crumb —
But never must I suck my thumb!

Hymns: *1* Hands to work and feet to run
2 The ink is black, the page is white

Prayer: Dear Father God, today help us to use our hands with gentleness, kindness and helpfulness, wherever they are needed. *Amen*

12 Just right!

When Goldilocks crept into the three bears' cottage, the first thing
she noticed was the table laid for breakfast. On the table were three
bowls of porridge. Father bear's plate was the biggest. The porridge
in his plate was still hot, but Goldilocks found that it tasted far too
salty for her liking. When she tried the porridge in mother bear's
plate, it had so much sugar sprinkled on it, that it was far too sweet
for her. Then she tried the porridge in baby bear's plate. It tasted
just right, so she ate it all up!

Like Goldilocks, we all need to learn what kind of food is just right
for us. If we don't have enough to eat, then our bodies grow thin
and weak — sadly, there are millions of people in the world who don't
have enough to eat. If we eat too much — lots of cakes and too many
sweets — then we grow fat and uncomfortable. Thousands of people
have made themselves ill by eating too much.

This is what happened to a girl who lived in India. Her mother
was so worried about her that she warned, 'If you keep on eating all
those sweets your teeth will go bad. You will grow so fat you won't
be able to run and play like your brothers and sisters, and all your
pretty clothes will be too tight for you to wear!'

But her warning made little difference. The girl loved everything
that was sweet. Whenever she tasted sweet food she always said,
'How delicious that was. I must have just a little more!'

In India at that time there lived a very clever and famous man
called Mohandas Gandhi. He was so wise that people often called him
'Mahatma' Gandhi. 'Mahatma' means 'Great Soul'. The worried
mother decided to take her daughter to visit him.

When they arrived she came straight to the point: 'Please,
Mahatma Gandhi, will you have a talk with my daughter? She is
eating far too many sweet things and they are bad for her. Nothing
I say makes any difference, but I'm sure she will listen to you.'

The wise man looked at the mother and daughter and smiled.
Then he looked thoughtful. 'Yes,' he replied, 'I will have a talk with
your daughter — but not today. Please bring her to see me in three
weeks' time and I'll see her then.'

Sure enough, in three weeks' time the woman and her daughter
were back again. True to his word Gandhi took the girl aside and
had a kindly talk with her. Later, when they were ready to leave,
the mother said, 'I thank you with all my heart for talking with my
daughter and giving her your wise advice. But please, Mahatma

Gandhi, do tell me one last thing. Why did you decide to wait three weeks before you would speak with her?'

Gandhi's eyes twinkled as he laughed and said, 'Ah well, I couldn't tell your daughter to give up sweets when I had the same problem myself. First of all I had to mend my own ways.'

Hymns: *1* See, here are red apples
2 When I needed a neighbour were you there?

Prayer: Dear Father God, we thank you for food that helps us to grow healthy and strong. We remember the people who work so that we may eat: farmworkers and fishermen . . . milkmen and bakers . . . mothers and fathers . . . the dinner ladies at school. We pray that all your children everywhere may have enough to eat today.

Amen

13 What is your favourite smell?

I know the food I like to taste,
I know what I like to see and hear;
I know the things I love to touch —
But when they asked me,
    What it was —
        I loved the best to smell?
        I couldn't really tell!

So, I asked . . .

    'Mum, what are your favourite smells?'
        She replied, 'The roast beef cooking in the oven,
            The washing fresh-dry off the line,
        Perfume on my handkerchief,
            A hot bath, with the scent of pine.'

    'Dad, what are your favourite smells?'
        He replied, 'Grass cuttings when I mow the lawn,
            Pickled onions, my glass of beer,
        Wood shavings, paint, my after-shave,
            Bacon and eggs when breakfast's near.'

'Granny, what are your favourite smells?'

    She replied, 'I love the smell of fresh mint sauce,
      Summer roses, marmalade making,
    Coffee brewing, winter fires,
      Scented soap and new bread baking.'

'Grandad, what are your favourite smells?'

    He replied, 'Your granny's scent, a bonfire burning,
      But when I was young and went to sea,
    The galley cooking, the foaming spray
      And my tot of rum, were the smells for me.'

Then . . .

    Brother Tom said, 'Bubble-gum',

    Sister Sue said, 'Play-dough',

    Auntie Ann thought, 'Strawberry jam',

    Cousin Jo said, 'I don't know!'

So I thought again — and remembered . . .

    My leather satchel, football boots,
      The swimming pool, railway stations,
    My favourite cheese, beans on toast,
      New clothes to wear on best occasions.

And strangely enough,
My favourite smell is —
The scent of the air in the early morning!
Now, I wonder what yours is?

Hymns: *1* At half-past three we go home to tea
2 For the beauty of the earth

Prayer: Dear Father God, we remember all the things that we enjoy. May we always be ready to share our blessings. *Amen*

14 Nugget and Larry

Everyone knows how important it is for us to look after our pets, but sometimes pets have to look after their owners. Guide dogs have been good friends to blind people for many years, but did you know that dogs can also help the deaf?

It's hard to imagine what it would be like not to hear voices, the birds singing, or music playing; not to hear the front door bell or the telephone; not to hear a car coming or the honking of a horn. The alarm clock wouldn't wake us and the kettle could sing until it boiled dry. A deaf mother isn't able to hear her baby cry, or the cooker buzzer.

This is the story of a dog called Nugget. Because her owner could no longer look after her, Nugget was given to an animal home. She waited patiently in her cage, hoping that someone would choose her to take home.

One day a visitor looked at all the dogs, and finally chose Nugget. She was a dog trainer who worked at a special college. Every day the trainers played with Nugget, until they were sure that she was friendly and would make a good and obedient pet. Then the work of teaching Nugget her new job began. Twice a day she was taken to a yard where she romped and played with her trainers. Then one of them would call out 'Sit!' and make a hand signal to show Nugget what to do.

'Sit Nugget,' 'Stay,' 'Come Nugget,' 'Down' — soon she had learned her first lessons.

After this, Nugget was taken with two trainers to part of the college where there was a flat, just like an ordinary home. One of the trainers pretended to be deaf and the other held Nugget on a long leash. They taught the dog to run to the 'deaf' trainer every time she heard certain sounds. When the alarm clock went off, Nugget went to lick her trainer's face, and tugged at the bedclothes until he got up. She also learned to run back and forward to the door when a bell was rung, until the 'deaf' trainer went with her to answer the doorbell.

'Good girl, good girl,' she was praised every time she did as she was told. 'Come on, Nugget, tell, tell,' they repeated to her as she learned a new command.

During Nugget's training a boy came to visit the college with his mother and father. His name was Larry. He was ten years old and very deaf. Even with a special hearing aid, he couldn't hear as well as other children. Larry looked at all the dogs very carefully, then he patted Nugget and chose her to be his pet.

He stayed at the college for two weeks, and in that time he and Nugget worked and played together every day. Larry learned how to give the hand signals that told Nugget what to do. He could make her sit, stay and come. Nugget learned to tell him when the door or telephone bell rang, and to wake him up in the morning. She even learned how to warn Larry if a car was coming.

At the end of the training Larry and Nugget went home. At last she was in a proper home again, and soon all the family loved her. As for Larry, he was overjoyed to have Nugget as his extra special pet and friend.

Poem: *Puppy and I*
I met a Horse as I went walking;
We got talking,
Horse and I.
   'Where are you going to, Horse, today?'
   (I said to the Horse as he went by).
   'Down to the village to get some hay.
   Will you come with me?' 'No, not I.'

I met some Rabbits as I went walking;
We got talking,
Rabbits and I.
   'Where are you going in your brown fur coats?'
   (I said to the Rabbits as they went by).
   'Down to the village to get some oats.
   Will you come with us?' 'No, not I.'

I met a Puppy as I went walking;
We got talking,
Puppy and I.
   'Where are you going this nice fine day?'
   (I said to the Puppy as he went by).
   'Up in the hills to roll and play.'
   'I'll come with you, Puppy,' said I.
A. A. Milne

Hymns: *1* To God who makes all lovely things
2 He gave me eyes so I could see

Prayer: Dear Father God, there are so many sounds we love to hear. We thank you for the gift of hearing. *Amen*

A project to train dogs for the deaf in the UK has been launched by PRO Dogs (Dogs for the Deaf Fund), in conjunction with The Royal National Institute for the Deaf.

15   A harvest holiday

Natalie and Tom had just come home from a holiday in France. They looked suntanned and happy as they told their grandmother about their adventures. 'Now you tell us about one of your holidays, Granny,' they said.

'Well, it's a long time ago now,' she began, 'right in the middle of the war and about this time of year, but it was a very unusual holiday. I was sixteen years old. We had just finished examinations and the bombing raids had quietened down. There was little chance of family holidays in wartime, because most of our fathers were soldiers, or sailors, or in the Air Force. It was a wonderful surprise one day when our headmaster said, "We're going to have a harvest camp. The farmers are needing help with the harvest and it will be a good working holiday for you big boys."

'You can imagine that we girls had something to say! We soon made it known that we would like to come as well. It seemed the farmers didn't want girls, but the headmaster said he would write to a chocolate factory close by to see if they needed us. Well, they didn't want us either, but in the end we were told we could come to camp for one week. If we found ourselves work in that time we could stay, otherwise — home we would have to go!

'It was a fine day when we arrived at the village station, about twenty miles away from home. We soon found the school on a hillside, where our camp was to be held. There were six of us girls and we were shown into the classroom that would be our dormitory. The chairs and desks had been piled on top of each other and pushed against the walls. On the floor lay six straw palliasses and we made up our beds with the cotton sheeting sleeping bags we'd brought from home, and the grey army blankets that lay waiting for us. Not at all grand — but we were excited just to be there. Before bedtime we explored a small pathway that led from the side of the school, through a gate and up to the field above. We watched the sun setting on the school, and the village in the distance.

'During the next week we set off on our bicycles to look for work. We explored country lanes and called at farms, asking if they wanted help with the harvest. At last one farmer said he could give us a week's work if we would weed his field of kale, which was covered with poppies and other wild flowers.

'Each day we cycled the five miles to the farm, which lay at the bottom of a steep winding hill. The lane was narrow and trees arched overhead — I can still remember the sunlight dappling through. It may seem a funny holiday to you, but we enjoyed our week of weed pulling.

'Another thing I remember well is the farmhouse, with the hens running and clucking outside, and the huge carthorses, and the cattle. I don't think any of us had been close enough to cows before to notice their big velvety eyes, and we loved to hear the farmer calling each one by name. At the end of the week we were paid our wage of one shilling an hour (five pence nowadays!) and said goodbye, thanking the farmer for his kindness.

'We were pleased to find out that our help was then needed on a fruit farm. We picked apples, filling cane baskets, while the men climbed wooden ladders to reach fruit that grew too high for us to reach. Then we changed to plum picking. The small trees were laden with fruit that year. In the early morning a pearly bloom covered the shining redness of the Victoria plums — they tasted as delicious as they looked!

'The days passed by so quickly. One day it was too wet to picnic outside, so at lunch-time we sheltered in a big barn. Pigs were rooting at one end, but we climbed on to bales of hay at the far end. We each had a quarter of a loaf of fresh white bread, butter we spread with our fingers, a chunk of cheese and an apple. At the end of our picnic we gave the pigs our apple-cores.

'On Sundays we went to church and some evenings were spent in the church hall playing table tennis. Afterwards we stayed to enjoy jam tarts and tea with the village people. We looked at the great bell in the church tower and wondered how it would sound. Everyone knew that if church bells sounded during the war, it would be a sign that the enemy had landed. But it didn't happen, and at the end of the war bells rang all across the country to tell everyone of peace!

'At the end of the six weeks we had a harvest home celebration. I don't know who did all the cooking for us, but I remember sitting down to a special meal. The hall was full — boys and girls, teachers and helpers, the farmers and the villagers. Everyone was happy. We sang and laughed and for a while forgot all about the war. We said a prayer to thank God for the harvest and for a happy harvest camp.

'Now,' finished Granny, 'that's my holiday story, and it's time for bed for you two!'

Poem: *Apple harvest*

Down in the orchard   Just ripe for the picking.
'Tis harvesting time   All juicy and sweet,
And up the tall ladders   So pretty to look at
The fruit pickers climb.   And lovely to eat!
                                         Helen Caddy

Hymns: *1* See, here are red apples
2 We plough the fields and scatter

Prayer: We thank you Father God for all the joys and blessings of the harvest. *Amen*

---

16 Naomi and Ruth

Autumn is a very colourful time of the year, as this poem says:

Autumn

Yellow the bracken,	Mist on the hillside,
Golden the sheaves,	Clouds grey and white.
Rosy the apples,	Autumn, good morning!
Crimson the leaves;	Summer, good night!

Florence Hoatson

Autumn is also harvest time, when farmers gather in their crops, and we pick apples, plums and pears if we have grown them in our gardens. This is a Bible story about harvest time, from the *Book of Ruth*.

A long, long time ago there was a very poor harvest in Bethlehem, so a man called Elimelech took his wife Naomi and their two sons to stay for a while in the country of Moab, where they found plenty of food and settled happily. In time Elimelech died, and the two sons married Moabite girls. Ten years later both Naomi's sons died, so she decided that she would like to go back to her old home in Bethlehem.

When she went to say goodbye to her sons' wives, the one called Ruth was so upset, she cried and pleaded with Naomi, 'Don't ask me to leave you. Please let me go with you. Wherever you go I will go. Wherever you live I will live. I want to take care of you and we will pray to God together.'

Naomi agreed, and the two women set off on their journey to Bethlehem. When they arrived, they found that it was harvest time. Many workers were busy gathering in barley and corn, and Ruth went into the fields of a man called Boaz to join the other women who were picking up the ears of barley dropped by the reapers. Later in the day, Boaz, the owner, came to visit the harvesters. When he saw Ruth he said to one of his servants, 'Who is that young woman? I haven't seen her before.'

31

One of his men told him about Ruth coming back from Moab with Naomi to look after her, and said how kind she had been.

Boaz came and spoke to Ruth. 'If you stay in my fields to glean, my servants will look after you. You may glean both barley and corn, and when you feel thirsty take a drink from our water jars. You will find them full of cool fresh water.'

Ruth was so pleased to hear this. 'Thank you Boaz, but I don't understand why you are being so kind to me when I'm a stranger to you!'

'I've heard all about you from my men,' Boaz said, 'and I know how good you have been to Naomi. You deserve to find kindness and God will reward you.'

How happy Naomi was when Ruth went home with her basket full of barley and corn. 'You have done well, Ruth. Now I shall be able to make flour for our bread.'

Ruth told Naomi all about the kindness of Boaz, and the two women settled down peacefully in Bethlehem. It was a happy day for Naomi when Boaz married Ruth, and when they had a baby son, Naomi helped to look after him.

Hymns: *1* See, here are red apples
2 All things bright and beautiful

Prayer: God paints the autumn leaves,
And clothes the moors with heather,
He fills the fields with golden corn,
And sends the sunny weather.
O God is great, and God is good,
Then let us praise him as we should.

Amen

The sequel to this Hebrew legend is that the son of Boaz and Ruth, named Obed, was the grandfather of David who slew the Philistine, Goliath.

Ruth 1–4

17 United Nations Day

All friends like to talk together and sometimes they even enjoy an argument, but if they really start to quarrel or fight, that's when the trouble begins! As in this poem:

Two little kittens

Two little kittens
One stormy night,
Began to quarrel
And then to fight.

One had a mouse
And the other had none;
And that was the way
The quarrel began.

'I'll have that mouse,'
Said the bigger cat.
'You'll have that mouse?
We'll see about that!'

'I will have that mouse,'
Said the tortoise-shell;
And, spitting and scratching,
On her sister she fell.

I've told you before
'Twas a stormy night,
When these two kittens
Began to fight.

The old woman took
The sweeping broom,
And swept them both
Right out of the room.

The ground was covered
With frost and snow,
They had lost the mouse,
And had nowhere to go.

So they lay and shivered
Beside the door,
Till the old woman finished
Sweeping the floor.

And then they crept in
As quiet as mice,
All wet with snow
And as cold as ice.

They found it much better
That stormy night,
To lie by the fire,
Than to quarrel and fight.

Jane Taylor

In this poem two quite different creatures learn to live together peacefully and happily:

Rabbit and Lark

'Under the ground
  It's rumbly and dark
And interesting,'
  Said Rabbit to Lark.

Said Lark to Rabbit,
  'Up in the sky
There's plenty of room
  And it's airy and light.'

'Under the ground
  It's warm and dry.
Won't you live with me?'
  Was the Rabbit's reply.

'The air's so sunny.
  I wish you'd agree,'
Said the little Lark,
  'To live with me.'

But under the ground
  And up in the sky,
Larks can't burrow
  Nor Rabbits fly.

So Skylark over
  And Rabbit under,
They had to settle
  To live asunder.

And often these two friends
  Meet with a will
For a chat together
  On top of the hill.

James Reeves

We call the 24th of October United Nations Day, and today we remember all those who work for peace between the people of every nation.

Hymns: *1* The ink is black, the page is white
2 When I needed a neighbour were you there?
3 Kumbayah

Prayer: Dear Father God, teach the children of the world that it is better to love one another than to fight, so that wars may cease and friendship and peace may grow between all nations.   *Amen*

---

18   A good idea

It was one of those beautiful still autumn mornings when the sun, shining through the early morning mist, made everyone feel it was good to be alive. Simon kissed his mother goodbye when they reached the school gate and ran off in the direction of his classroom door.

'Good morning,' his mother greeted the mother of Simon's friend, Robert.

'Good morning, Mrs Stuart,' she replied. 'It's their big day today!'

Together the two mothers walked through the big glass doors at the front of the Infant School. They could hear music from the record player in the hall, and could smell school dinners being prepared as they passed by the kitchens. Inside the hall, the sun shone on the highly-polished wooden floor and the table of plants and flowers, which looked especially beautiful that morning.

It was Friday, the day when one of the classes took morning assembly and invited their families to join in. The parents chatted quietly until teachers and children began to come into the hall from their classrooms. Mrs Stuart had already heard from Simon that they were working on the theme of 'hands' that week, and she smiled when she looked at the frieze with all the hand-prints arranged on it. Simon and Robert had told her of the fun they'd had when painting their hands for the prints, and how difficult it had been to cut out the shapes properly.

Everyone listened as the children showed what their hands had made — pictures painted, cakes baked, models built, sewing stitched. They had also made puppets, written stories about them, and used hand-spans to measure length. The class sang a song they had learned especially for that morning, and a few of the children read prayers they had written. To finish the assembly the children and their visitors sang the hymn: 'Hands to work and feet to run'.

Mrs Stuart looked thoughtful as she left the school. She had an idea and wanted to share it with Robert's mother. The next week the two mothers went to see Mrs Mills, the headteacher. 'We do enjoy sharing the children's assemblies,' they told her. 'We thought it might be a good idea if we did an assembly for the children next time!'

Mrs Mills said, 'What a wonderful idea. We've never had this happen before. I'm quite sure the children would enjoy it.'

When the next Friday came round, eight mothers arrived early and arranged tables in the front of the hall. Simon's mother had brought an orange washing-up bowl with a few cups and saucers, a small dish-mop and a tea cloth; Robert's mother came with a big shopping basket full of groceries; another mother brought a mixing bowl with sugar, flour, eggs, butter and all the other things needed to make a cake; yet another brought her laundry basket, some clothes, washing powder, pegs and an iron. One girl's mum brought a broom and a big yellow duster; and another had her sewing basket with scissors, needles and thread.

Teachers and children came to sit in the hall and looked with great interest at the mothers, who were all wearing huge aprons. The one with the broom had tied a bright red handkerchief over her hair. The children listened carefully as the mothers told them all about the things that happened at home during the school day. They sent love from the mums and dads who couldn't come that day because they were at work. Then they took turns to recite a line from a poem specially written for that assembly, and they all mimed the actions:

'When you are away, I'm busy all day!

There are dishes to wash and beds to make,
The shopping to do, then perhaps bake a cake.
The clothes must be washed and then ironed too,
There is plenty of dusting and sweeping to do.

When you are at school I don't read a book,
For there are rooms to be tidied and lunches to cook.
Then there's library duty and things to repair.
We work hard at home, when you are not there.'

At bedtime that night Simon said, 'We liked your assembly, Mum. Robert says, when will you do it again?'

Hymns: *1* Daisies are our silver, buttercups our gold
2 Hands to work and feet to run

Prayer: Thank you for the world so sweet.
Thank you for the food we eat.
Thank you for the birds that sing.
Thank you God for everything.
And thank you especially God for our mothers.

Amen

---

19 Fit for a Queen

'There's no place like home!' These are the words of an old song, and we all know just what they mean. Home may be a big house or a small cottage. Some people live in a flat, others in a caravan or even a boat. Then there are those whose home is a palace, as in our story.

A very long time ago the city of Agra was a busy place. There were grand houses with lovely gardens; big parks with fountains; and broad roads which brought travellers from Persia, Arabia, China and Europe to visit the famous markets. The many noblemen lived in brick and sandstone homes, and at royal Fort Agra the Emperor lived in his palace.

The fort was built on the banks of the river Yamuna and was almost like a small town itself. It was ten kilometres across, with green lawns, marble fountains, hanging gardens and waterways. There were grand buildings with balconies ornamented with rubies and other precious gems, and the ceilings were said to be solid gold. High walls and two deep moats ran all round the fort, and the only way to enter was over a huge drawbridge guarded by soldiers.

On certain days the court ladies held a bazaar, and princes and noblemen would come to buy silks, jewellery, oils and bangles. It was on such a day that a beautiful young girl called Arjumand Banu Begum was busily selling bangles, rings and trinkets to the visitors. She didn't know that Prince Khurram, the Emperor's son, had decided to visit the bazaar. He rode into the fort at the head of twenty Arabian thoroughbred horses that were bedecked in rich saddlecloths. Dismissing his bodyguard, he told the court trumpeters to be silent. 'I don't want the whole world to know that I am here!'

The handsome prince strolled round the bazaar, looking at the goods for sale and sometimes stopping to speak to friends. At one of the tents he was surprised to see a lovely young girl telling a customer that he couldn't buy a certain ring, because it would cost one hundred gold coins.

The prince said to her, 'Let *me* see the ring!'

Arjumand stared in astonishment at the richly-dressed prince with his jewelled turban. Her eyes flashed with pride.

'This piece of glass will cost you one hundred gold coins — buy it if you will . . .,' she laughed.

Khurram smiled at her and took the golden coins from his purse. Before the amazed girl could open her mouth he took the ring from her and walked off saying, 'You will smile upon me one day when I slip this ring on your finger, along with rubies and diamonds.'

Prince Khurram did not forget the beautiful Arjumand. He learned that she was the Prime Minister's daughter, and before long he had won the Emperor's permission to marry her.

'Let permission be granted, but you may not marry until the time is right and the astrologers give a proper date,' the Emperor decreed.

Neither the prince nor Arjumand realised that it would be five years before the stars were in the correct position for the marriage to take place!

According to Muslim custom, the wedding was at the home of Arjumand's father. It was a day never to be forgotten. Arjumand was dressed in beautiful robes that had taken four years to make. Scented and bejewelled, she waited for her prince. The royal wedding procession was on its way. Trumpets and drums played a marriage tune, torches lit the way, and soldiers on horseback kept the crowds from coming too close.

Holy men and Muslim priests led the procession, while clowns and acrobats turned cartwheels and played tricks all along the way. In the middle of all this rode Prince Khurram on his white Arabian mare, wearing a gown studded with jewels and a turban that sparkled with emeralds, rubies and diamonds.

After the wedding and the sumptuous feast that followed, the Emperor said, 'I love my new daughter-in-law dearly. She is like the moon and the stars in her beauty and I would like to honour her with a new name. From this day on she will be called Mumtaz Mahal or "The Chosen One of the Palace".'

Prince Khurram and his wife lived happily in their palace for many years. The prince grew into a wise man, and Mumtaz Mahal became the mother of twelve children. There were many servants to care for them and they were surrounded with riches and splendour, but no man, woman or child ever visited their home without being given whatever food or money they needed.

When the old Emperor died, Prince Khurram was crowned Emperor of India. As a special honour he was given a new name — Shah Jahan or "King of the World" — and his Queen, of course, was the beautiful Mumtaz Mahal.

Saying: Mid pleasures and palaces though we may roam,
Be it ever so humble, there's no place like home.

Hymns: *1* Can you count the stars?
2 At half-past three we go home to tea

Prayer: Dear Father God, we thank you for our homes and our families. Please help us always to do our share in making home a really happy place. *Amen*

The coronation of Prince Khurram was on the 4th of February, 1628. Mumtaz Mahal died two years later, after giving birth to a daughter. Shah Jahan was heartbroken and determined to build a fitting memorial to her. He built the Taj Mahal — later to be known as one of the seven wonders of the world.

Taj Mahal, Agra, India.   *Photograph: Topham*

38

20 Going home for Christmas

It's time to go home for Christmas, children! All over the country people will be hurrying home for Christmas. Some will be walking home along darkened country lanes, others will be on buses going through brightly-lit streets. Some families will look out from their living-room windows on to winter gardens, and others will gaze down on to the bustling city from their high-rise flats.

So many people, so many homes, as in these poems:

God's lovely things
God gives my home — a place to stay
And laugh, and dream, and work, and play
The pleasant rooms and windows wide
And cosy, rosy fireside;

And books to read, and folks to love me,
And his good care to watch above me.
It's like a song a person sings —
God gives so many happy things!   *N. B. Turner*

Our street
Our street is not a posh place,
Say the mums in curlers, dads in braces, kids in nothing.

Our street is not a quiet place,
Says our football match, our honking bikes, our shouts.

Our street is not a tidy place,
Says the lolly wrappers, chippie bags, and written-on walls.

Our street is not a lazy place,
Say the car-washing dads, clothes-washing mums, and
marbling boys.

Our street is not a new place,
Say the paint-peeled doors, pavements worn, and crumbly walls.

Our street is not a green place,
Say the pavements grey, forgotten gardens, lines of cars.

But our street is the best,
Says me.
          L. T. Baynton

We remember the travellers of so long ago . . .

'Can we make your inn our home for tonight?' asked Mary and Joseph, so tired after their long journey to Bethlehem.

The kindly inn-keeper replied, 'There's no room in the inn, I'm sorry to say, but the stable is warm and dry and you're welcome — come on in.'

So let's go home for Christmas, and may all our homes be filled with happiness at this time of celebration.

Comment by a child of refugee parents.
'Home? Yes, we have a home, but no house to put round it.'

Hymns: *1* Away in a manger
2 The Virgin Mary had a baby boy

Prayer: Dear Father God, we remember the birthday of Jesus and say thank you Lord. All over the country, all over the world, people are hurrying home for Christmas. We pray that every home will share in the happiness, peace and joy of this special time.   *Amen*

---

21   **A Happy New Year!**

'Happy New Year!' everyone says, and we wonder what the new year will *give to us*. We hope for good health ... new friends perhaps . . . interesting things to learn . . . new games to play. If we're lucky, there will be holidays to look forward to, as well as working days. Maybe there will be some sad days, but we hope for many more happy days.

But when we say 'Happy New Year' it's a good idea to think — what can *we give* to this brand new year? Will we be just a little quicker to notice anyone who needs a helping hand? Could we try just a little harder in our work and in our play? Will we give a little time to cheer up someone who is sad? Will we sometimes stop and say 'Thank you God', when we look at the beautiful world we live in? Here is a poem about the year in front of us:

January brings the snow,
Makes our feet and fingers glow.

February brings the rain,
Thaws the frozen lake again.

March brings breezes, loud and shrill,
To stir the dancing daffodil.

April brings the primrose sweet,
Scatters daisies at our feet.

May brings flocks of pretty lambs,
Skipping by their fleecy dams.

June brings tulips, lilies, roses,
Fills the children's hands with posies.

Hot July brings cooling showers,
Apricots and gillyflowers.

August brings the sheaves of corn,
Then the harvest home is borne.

Warm September brings the fruit,
Sportsmen then begin to shoot.

Fresh October brings the pheasant,
Then to gather nuts is pleasant.

Dull November brings the blast,
Then the leaves are whirling fast.

Chill December brings the sleet,
Blazing fire and Christmas treat.

Sarah Coleridge

Someone once said: 'Remember that today is the first day of the rest of your life.' This year let's try and make every day a good day.

Hymns: *1* Day by day
2 All things bright and beautiful

Prayer: We thank you Father God for all our blessings. Please keep us safe in your love, today and all through this new year.

Amen

22   My Monday morning mood

'Twas on a Monday morning, my mummy said to me,
  'The baby isn't well today, the doctor we must see.
'I'll catch the bus at half-past nine, if you will help me to —'
  'I can't, I'm tired, let daddy help, I want to play with Hugh!'

'Twas on a Tuesday morning, my brother came to me,
  'Let's give our gran a nice surprise, she's coming home for tea.
'We'll pick some flowers and write a card and say with love from us —'
  'Not me,' I said, 'I'm busy now, I'm playing with my bus.'

41

'Twas on a Wednesday morning, my friend knocked on the door,
  'My puppy's lost, I've looked around the house and what is more
'He isn't in the garden, let's go and search the park —'
  'I'll not go with you, can't you see, I'm playing Noah's Ark.'

'Twas on a Thursday morning, when teacher said to us,
  'The playground looks untidy, let's pick these papers up.'
The children gathered up the litter, and put it in the bin.
  I hid away, pretended blind, *my* help they wouldn't win.

'Twas on a Friday morning, the Oxfam man spoke to mummy,
  'For the poor and sick in India, we really need some money.'
'We'll gladly help,' my mother said, 'we'll give you what we can.'
  I wish she'd given that to *me*, and not the Oxfam man.

'Twas on a Saturday morning, there was something wrong that day —
  My mum was cross, my brother mad, no friends had come to play!
'But why so sad, son?' father asked. I tried so hard to say.
  'Life's better, son, if we try to help each other every day.'

'Twas on a Sunday morning, I was as happy as could be,
  We tidied up the breakfast things, my brother, dad and me.
My friends were glad to see me, in church I said a prayer —
  'I thank you God for everything, and everybody, everywhere!'

Sayings: One of the most famous sayings in the world is found in many different religions, in words such as:
  Always treat others as you would like them to treat you.

Other old sayings are:
A friend in need is a friend indeed.
A little help is worth a lot of pity.
Every little helps.

Bible story: The Good Samaritan *Luke* 10.30–37

Music: Grieg, *Peer Gynt suite* (*Morning mood*)

Hymns: *1* Thank you for every good new morning
2 Morning has broken, like the first morning
3 Jesus' hands were kind hands

Prayer: Dear God, each day may we find a way to be kind to the people we meet, especially if anyone is in trouble and needs our help. *Amen*

23   The missing voice

On some winter days the land is covered with a silent blanket of snow, or shimmers white with frost and ice. Then there are other days when great black clouds hang heavily until — it is just as if the heavens have opened — lightning flashes, thunder roars and the rain pours down. You know what a noise thunder can make!

One of the favourite creatures of African and Caribbean folk stories is the spider Anansi. People call him Brer Anansi, which means Brother Anansi. In this story he has an adventure with Mr Thunder himself.

One morning Brer Anansi woke up early and poked his head out of his tree house. What a shock he had! It was the greatest shock of his entire life. He was trembling with fright, for standing at the bottom of the tree was Mr Thunder. How Brer Anansi wished he were somewhere else. He remembered the times when he had tried to trick Mr Thunder, and his many knees started knocking together and his teeth began to chatter. When Mr Thunder beckoned a finger at Brer Anansi he nearly died with fright. He couldn't possibly go down. Mr Thunder beckoned again, and this time Brer Anansi found enough courage to step forward. He held on to his tree rope and reluctantly slid down, bit by bit.

Brer Anansi stood shivering at Mr Thunder's feet. What big feet, what a big body, and that mouth . . .! To his surprise, Mr Thunder started writing in a notebook. What was going on? Mr Thunder held out the book. The spider stretched out a shaking hand and took it.

He read, 'I have lost my voice! Brer Anansi, you have got to help me find it.'

He just couldn't believe his eyes. No wonder Mr Thunder was quiet. It was almost unbelievable, the great Mr Thunder without a voice!

Then he had a terrible thought. Supposing this was a trick. Mr Thunder took the book and wrote, 'This is no trick. I lost my voice last night in Echo Valley in the next country and I can't find it. If you help me to find it, I'll give you anything you want.'

Brer Anansi didn't feel frightened any more, but he had to do some quick thinking.

'If you will give me a dozen thunderbolts I'll find your voice for you,' he said.

It was a wonderful chance for Brer Anansi. With twelve thunderbolts he could drop one on his old enemies Brer Bear and Brer

Rabbit, and that would take care of them. The other eleven could be used on any animals who opposed him when he appointed himself the Emperor of Animal Land.

'Mr Thunder, worry no more. I, Brer Anansi, will help you. Come back in a few days and I shall have your voice ready for you.'

Mr Thunder left with a big smile on his face. Brer Anansi realised that Mr Thunder had made himself hoarse shouting all night in Echo Valley and he was sure his voice would soon come back. But when Mr Thunder returned he was no longer smiling, in fact his face was black.

'No voice yet? Dear me, show me your tongue, Mr Thunder,' requested Brer Anansi hastily. 'As I thought, one more day will do it. You come back tomorrow, and don't forget the thunderbolts.'

Mr Thunder agreed to this in writing, but the next day Brer Anansi looked out from his tree house and saw Mr Thunder storming along without the thunderbolts.

'There is only one thing to do now,' he thought, and ran away as quickly as possible to hide until Mr Thunder had forgotten all about him.

And did Mr Thunder recover his voice? You may be sure he did. Listen when the sky is cloudy and it rains a lot. You will be sure to hear him, and you may even see a thunderbolt.

Brer Anansi never forgot his adventure with Mr Thunder. He told his friends:
'When lightning flashes
And Thunder roars,
Take my advice
And stay indoors!'

Bible story: When the friends of Jesus were sad or frightened, he said to them: 'Peace is what I leave with you . . . do not be worried or upset; do not be afraid.' *John* 14.27

Hymns: *1* God who made the earth
2 I love the sun

Prayer: We thank you, loving Father, for all your tender care;
For food and clothes and shelter, and all the world so fair.
Amen

24 **A friend for Zacchaeus**

This is the story of a rich man called Zacchaeus, who lived in a big house in the town of Jericho. He had fine clothes to wear, servants to wait on him and plenty of food to eat. He was a tax collector, and when people came to him to pay their taxes, he often took more than he should have done, and kept some for himself. The people guessed that Zacchaeus wasn't honest and they didn't like him. So, without any friends to be kind to him and keep him company, Zacchaeus was an unhappy and lonely man.

One day he heard that Jesus was coming to visit their town. He had heard so many stories about Jesus. Some people said he was a clever teacher; others said he was a kind man, friendly to everyone — even to people who had done wrong. Others said that their friends had been ill and Jesus had made them well again.

'I want to see this Jesus,' said Zacchaeus. So he went out to the road where the crowds were waiting. Everyone seemed to have the same idea. The town was packed with people and there was a great feeling of excitement, as the word spread that Jesus would soon be with them. He tried hard to get to the front of the crowd but no one would let him through, and he was such a small man that he couldn't see over their heads.

Suddenly he had an idea. 'I know what to do,' he thought.

There was a sycomore tree by the side of the road with widely spreading branches. Zacchaeus scrambled up the tree and lay along a strong branch that hung over the pathway. He lay there quietly — no one had noticed him — and he watched as Jesus and his friends slowly made their way through the crowds. So many people wanted to speak to them and it seemed a long time before Jesus arrived. Then Zacchaeus had such a surprise that he nearly fell from the tree.

Jesus had stopped right below the sycomore tree and he called out, 'Zacchaeus, come down quickly. I must come and stay with you today in your house.'

Zacchaeus slid down to the ground. 'My home isn't far from here, Master,' he said. 'The servants will prepare the best room for you.'

That night Jesus listened while Zacchaeus told him how greedy he had been and how unhappy life was without any friends. Outside, the people couldn't understand why Jesus should visit a man like Zacchaeus, and they began to grumble. But the next morning as Jesus was leaving, the crowds heard Zacchaeus make a promise: 'Here and now I will give away half of all I have, and if I have cheated anyone I will pay him back four times over.'

Stone capital depicting Zacchaeus in the tree.
Photograph: Picturepoint – London

Zacchaeus knew he had found a friend in Jesus. He kept his promise and before long he had many more friends, and at last he was a happy man. *Luke 19.1–10*

Song: (to the traditional melody of *Old King Cole*)
Zacchaeus was a very little man
  And a very little man was he,
He climbed into a sycamore tree
  So Jesus he could see.
And when Jesus came along
  He looked up into the tree.
He said, 'Zacchaeus come right down
  For I'm coming to your house for tea.'

Hymns: *1* When I needed a neighbour were you there?
2 Daisies are our silver, buttercups our gold
3 Who's that sitting in the sycamore tree?

Sung prayer: Jesus, friend of little children,
      Be a friend to me;
    Take my hand and ever keep me
      Close to thee.

    Never leave me nor forsake me,
      Ever be my friend;
    For I need thee from life's dawning
      To its end.

25 Pancake racing

Long ago at this time of year, many people would fast before Easter. First they prepared a feast to use up any spare food in their larders. Eggs, fat and flour were made into pancakes, and sometimes pancake races would be held. This tradition is still practised in some places, as in this story:

Marcus, who was five, lived in a village in Hertfordshire. He had been going to school for nearly two terms, and his teacher said he was working very well.

When she heard this, his mother told him, 'When half-term holiday comes, I'll take you and baby Shula to visit Granny and Grandpa, for a treat.'

This pleased Marcus. His grandparents lived on the Isle of Wight, so the journey seemed a great adventure. His mother drove the car to Lymington and then on to the ferry-boat. When all the cars were on board the ramp was raised and the ferry glided slowly out of the river. They passed the marina, where hundreds of sailing boats were moored, and sailed out across the Solent to the harbour at Yarmouth. Marcus stood on the deck as the boat neared the island, and he could see the house where his grandparents lived.

At breakfast the next morning Granny told them about the pancake races in the village square at eleven o'clock that day. Everyone decided that it would be fun to go and join in. Shula was strapped in her push-chair and they set off in great excitement. The square was crowded with people — children and grown-ups of all ages, the village policeman, shopkeepers, photographers and the Rector of the local church.

At exactly eleven o'clock a man with a loud-hailer explained the races. There would be different races for boys and girls of each age group, also races for mothers, fathers and 'old crocks'. Every runner would carry a frying-pan with a pancake in it, and the pancake had to be tossed into the air three times during the race. The competitors were to run down the square, round a man wearing a huge hat, then back again.

The first race was for boys of Marcus's age. He didn't know any of the other children and suddenly felt very shy.

His mother said, 'Don't worry if you don't want to run, Marcus! We'll watch the other boys.'

Everyone shouted and cheered, especially when some boys dropped their pancakes and had to stop to pick them up. All the runners were given a sweet as their reward. Even Marcus got one, because a big boy called Timothy gave him the sweet he had won! In the ladies' race Marcus's mother won a wooden spoon and a lemon. Granny won the old crock's race, and her prize was a wooden spoon.

Everyone enjoyed themselves, but all too soon the pancake races were over for another year, and the square was quiet again.

When Marcus was back at school he told his teacher and friends all about the pancake races. He showed them a newspaper picture of his mother tossing her pancake into the air. 'One day,' he announced, 'I want to go back to the Isle of Wight and I *will* run in the pancake race!'

Poem: *The pancake*
Mix a pancake
Stir a pancake
Pop it in the pan.
Fry the pancake
Toss the pancake
Catch it if you can!
Christina Rossetti

Hymns: *1* Hands to work and feet to run
2 Thank you for every good new morning

Prayer: Whatever we do today, dear God, help us to do our best
and help others in every way we can.   *Amen*

'Shrove' means to be forgiven. It has been a Christian tradition to go to
church on Shrove Tuesday to pray for forgiveness before commencing the
Lenten fast prior to Easter.

The pancake story is based on the 1980 races in Yarmouth, Isle of Wight.

26 A B C

Twenty-six letters
Twenty-six cards in half a pack;
Twenty-six weeks in half a year;
Twenty-six letters dressed in black
In all the words you will ever hear.

In King, Queen, Ace and Jack,
In London, lucky, lone and lack,
January, April, fortify, fix,
You'll never find more than twenty-six.

Think of the beautiful things you see
On mountain, riverside, meadow and tree.
How many their names are, but how small
The twenty-six letters that spell them all.
James Reeves

A good way to start each day is to think about all the blessings we have — all the good things we enjoy. Let's think of some in alphabetical order:

A — an apple from the apple tree,
B — for baby, book and bee.
C — a cat, cook, cake and cress,
D — a dog, a doll and dress.
E — an egg for everyone,
F — for father, friend and fun.
G — gorgeous girls and green the grass is,
H — is for happy, and horses and harness.
I — iris, or the colour of indigo,
J — jump for joy at the circus show.
K — a kitten so playful and small,
L — for a lighthouse strong and tall.
M — is for mother — that everyone knows!
N — is for no one, nothing and nose.
O — for oranges — juicy and sweet,
P — we play with our pets, but not in the street.
Q — for our Queen, long may she reign,
R — for red roses — it's summer again.
S — the sun that shines for all to see,
T — for teachers, toys and tea.
U — the umbrella shelters us under its dome,
V — a vase of violets looks pretty at home.
W — wellington boots for a winter day,
X — a xylophone on which to play.
Y — for yoghurt, yellow and *you*,
Z — a zebra at the zoo.

All the letters of the alphabet,
To remind us of blessings,
In case we forget.

Hymns: *1* For the beauty of the earth
2 Give me joy in my heart

Prayer: Dear Father God, we think about all the blessings we enjoy, and remember that there are many people who are not as lucky as us. Help us to do what we can to make others happy today.   *Amen*

27 Margarete's teddy bears

One toy that everyone enjoys is a teddy bear. Bears come in all sizes and colours and are so friendly and cheerful, they are always a favourite.

But who made the first one; what is teddy's story? Well, it started like this. In Germany there was a little girl called Margarete Steiff who became very ill. It was a long time before she felt better and then she found she couldn't walk. But Margarete was a brave and determined girl, and although she had to sit in a wheelchair she loved to read, play games and sew. When she grew up she was so clever at sewing that she made clothes for people in the town.

On a quiet day, with little work to do, Margarete found some pretty pieces of material and cut out a small elephant shape. Carefully she sewed the elephant together, then padded him and sewed on eyes. Margarete showed the toy to a young girl who came to visit her that day.

'What a beautiful elephant, you are very clever!' exclaimed the delighted child.

When Margarete saw how the baby elephant had pleased her visitor she made more animals — tigers, lions, cats, dogs and horses — and she gave them as presents to children she knew.

Soon people were asking to buy her toys and Margarete started a small toy factory in her room. She taught other people how to make the animals, and paid them for their work. These toys soon became so popular that the workers needed more space, and a bigger building was found. Buyers were coming from all over Germany, from England and even from America to order Margarete's toys.

One day her nephew arrived with a present. 'Auntie Margarete, I've been drawing pictures of bears at the zoo. I thought you would like a little bear, so I've made one for you,' he said to her.

What a lovely surprise! Margarete looked carefully at the bear, to see if she could make a toy just like it. The factory began to make bears, but somehow no one was keen to buy them. So she changed the pattern. The bear was made a little thinner, and just a little softer. His arms and legs and head moved like the first bear, but now he looked more lovable. He was also cheaper to buy.

When an American saw the new bears he said, 'They're beautiful. Just the kind of toy I'm looking for — I'll have three thousand, please!'

It was hard work making three thousand bears. For months the factory had to work from early in the morning until late at night, but at last three thousand bears were ready to travel to America.

At that time the American President was Theodore Roosevelt, and because his name was rather long, all his friends called him Teddy.

His daughter was soon to be married, so the President was holding a celebration party at the White House. Almost everything was ready, but the man who was making the arrangements for the President was still looking for one last thing. He needed table decorations and he desperately wanted to find something new, an idea no one had ever used before. One day he saw some bears from Margarete Steiff's factory in a shop window and thought how unusual they looked. Suddenly he had an idea, the bears would be just the thing . . .!

When the wedding guests arrived at the White House they found the tables decorated with bears — all dressed in different costumes. There was a camping bear in wellingtons and smock, standing beside his tent; a fishing bear stood with rod and line in his paw; a soldier bear held a rifle — everyone exclaimed how attractive and interesting the tables looked.

'What sort of bears are they, Teddy?' someone asked Theodore Roosevelt.

'Well, I'm afraid they're new to me,' he admitted with a laugh.

Then a guest added in fun, 'They must be teddy bears.'

Next day the newspapers were full of stories about the President's wedding party and the teddy bears. After this, Margarete Steiff's toy factory in Germany received so many orders for bears, they had to build an even bigger factory.

Teddy bears by the hundreds, thousands and even millions are now made all over the world — to the delight of so many children — and (don't tell anyone) they please many grown-ups too!

Hymns: *1* Hands to work and feet to run
2 The sun that shines across the sea

Prayer: We remember people like Margarete Steiff, who overcome their special problems with brave hearts and real courage. Dear God, we thank you for all our many blessings.   *Amen*

28   An unusual census

'1, 2, 3, 4, 5 — once I caught a fish alive. 6, 7, 8, 9, 10 — then I let it go again.' The children in Peter's class loved to count. Sometimes they counted forward and sometimes they counted backward: 10, 9, 8, 7, 6, 5, 4, 3, 2, 1, zero. Some children could count backward as quickly as forward. They didn't always count in ones either — 2, 4, 6, 8, 10 — nearly everyone could count in twos to one hundred, and some went even further.

Next the teacher, Mrs Wright, taught them to count in fives and in tens. That was easy, backward and forward, but they found it more difficult to do the same in threes. They counted the scissors in the scissor-box, the milk bottles in the crate, and of course they counted the children in class every day — how many girls, how many boys, and how many altogether.

One beautiful spring morning Mrs Wright said, 'I think it would be fun to do our counting outside today. We'll go out to the school field and we'll do a traffic census for half an hour. Peter, give out these pieces of paper and I'll show you all how we will work.'

The pages were divided into four columns. One was headed *Cars*; another *Lorries and Vans*; the third said *Cycles and Motorbikes*; but the fourth column was empty.

Mrs Wright said, 'You may think of something else you would like to count, and you can put it in the last column.'

The children all thought it was a great idea to practise counting outside. They put on their jackets and raced to the wire fence which separated the school field from the busy main road.

'Don't start until I tell you,' Mrs Wright said. 'It's important that we time our counting properly.'

Exactly at ten o'clock she said 'Go,' and the children settled down to count. They had learned to put a line on the paper, like a figure 1, every time something passed. Four lines side by side in the *Car* column meant that four cars had gone by. When the fifth car passed they put a line through the other four, crossing them out. At the end it would be easy to count the little blocks of five and add on any extra ones.

Sometimes cars came quickly one after the other. It was hard work to make sure that each one had its line, especially when there were a few lorries to count, not to mention the cyclists and a man on a motorbike.

Peter's friend Jonathan covered his paper with his hand. 'I know what I'm putting in my spare column,' he whispered.

Sarah and Jane did the same: then everyone thought it was a good idea to keep their fourth column a secret. The half hour passed very quickly and it didn't seem long before Mrs Wright stopped them.

Back in the classroom and talking about their traffic census, the secrets of the fourth column soon came out. Sarah and Jane and some others had counted the people who walked by on the pavement. Jenny and Jonathan had both spotted magpies and gulls swooping across the road. Peter was the only one who had noticed a small aeroplane fly over, while everyone else was busy watching the road.

They were then shown how to make a histogram, with coloured boxes of different lengths to represent the 'traffic' in that half hour. Their census showed 28 cars, 15 lorries and vans, 4 cycles, 1 motorbike, 9 pedestrians, 4 birds and 1 aeroplane!

Afterwards Mrs Wright reminded the children about the census that had caused Mary and Joseph to travel to Bethlehem on the night that Jesus was born. She also told them about the census in our country which happens every ten years in the month of April — when every man, woman and child is counted.

'I remember the census in 1951, 1961, 1971 and 1981,' said Mrs Wright. 'Will you remember the next one in 19 . . . ?'

Quickly the class got the answer — '1991.'

'Well done, what a clever class I have,' smiled Mrs Wright.

Peter looked at the big clock on the classroom wall. 'One minute to go,' he thought. '10, 9, 8, 7, 6, 5, 4, 3, 2, 1 — there's the bell for playtime!'

Hymns: *1* Can you count the stars?
2 At half-past three we go home to tea

Prayer: Father God, we thank you for our teachers and for all the work and play we share in school. Help us to count our blessings today and every day. *Amen*

Bible story: Mary and Joseph travel to Bethlehem *Luke 2.1–7*

29 A teacher called Jesus

When Jesus was about thirty years old, he gathered around him twelve special friends and with their help began to teach people the good news that God loved them. Sometimes he spoke to them in the synagogue, sometimes people crowded around him on the hillside or by the side of the great lake. He taught them the way that God wanted them to live.

They listened as he said, 'With God all things are possible,' and they watched while he made a lame man walk and blind men see again. The Bible tells many stories of men, women and children who were healed by Jesus.

Mothers brought their babies and young children. They struggled to get near Jesus, so that he could touch the children and bless them. When the friends of Jesus noticed how people were pushing through to him, they frowned and looked very cross.

Jesus called across to them, 'You must let the little children come to me, and you must never stop them coming. The Kingdom of Heaven belongs to little children like these.'

One day Jesus said, 'Listen. God wants you to treat others exactly as you would like them to treat you. If you love only those people who love you, that's easy, anyone can do that. If you help only the people who help you, that's easy, anyone can do that. And, if you lend something to someone who is sure to pay you back, why should you receive a blessing? No. What you must do is this. Love and help everyone, even the people who are not your friends. You must be full of goodness, like your Father in Heaven.'

Sometimes Jesus told stories to help people understand what he was teaching. He said, 'If you listen to what I tell you, you are like a man who builds his house on a foundation of rock. When the floods come, his house will stay strong. If you don't listen and won't try to do as I tell you, then you are like a man who builds his house on sand. When the floods come, his house will tumble down.'

One day, after talking to the crowds, Jesus and his friends set off to Capernaum. A Roman officer lived there, a centurion in charge of one hundred Roman soldiers. His servant, whom he loved very much, was ill and about to die. When the officer heard that Jesus was coming he sent some Jewish elders to ask Jesus to heal his servant. These men said to Jesus, 'This is a good man who deserves your help. He loves our people and has even built a synagogue for us.'

So Jesus went with the elders, but as they came near the house, the centurion sent out some friends to say, 'Sir, don't trouble yourself. I don't deserve to have you come into my house. Just give the order and my servant will get well. I know how to obey orders from my commanding officer, and my soldiers in turn obey me. If I order this one 'go', he goes; and if I order that one 'come', he comes.'

When Jesus heard this, he was amazed. 'I tell you,' he said, 'I have never found faith like this!' The messengers went back to the officer's house and they found the servant quite well again.

Hymns: *1* Jesus, friend of little children
2 Jesus' hands were kind hands

Prayer: Jesus taught the people, 'When you pray, say this:
Father, may your holy name be honoured;
May your kingdom come.
Give us day by day the food we need.
Forgive us our sins, for we forgive
everyone who does us wrong.
And do not bring us to hard testing.'

Bible stories: Jesus heals the sick *Matthew* 8.14–16; 9.27–31; 15.29–31 *Luke* 4.38–41
Jesus and the children *Matthew* 19.13–15 *Luke* 18.15–17
Love your enemies *Matthew* 5.43–48 *Luke* 6.27–28; 32–36
The house built on rock *Matthew* 7.24–27 *Luke* 6.47–49
The centurion's servant *Matthew* 8.5–13 *Luke* 7.1–10
The Lord's prayer *Matthew* 6.9–13 *Luke* 11.1–4

30 I want to be new

Most days we do the same kind of thing. We get up, have breakfast, come to school. We work a little, play a little, eat a little, drink a little. . . . Did you ever get the feeling you would like to be new? Did you want to look new, feel new, meet exciting people, and perhaps do exciting things? Well, listen to this tale.

The new duckling
'I want to be new,' said the duckling.
  'O, ho!' said the wise old owl,
While the guinea-pig cluttered off chuckling
  To tell all the rest of the fowl.

'I should like a more elegant figure,'
  That child of a duck went on.
'I should like to grow bigger and bigger,
  Until I could swallow a swan.

'I won't be the bond-slave of habit,
  I won't have those webs on my toes,
I want to run round as a rabbit,
  A rabbit as red as a rose.

'I don't want to waddle like mother,
  Or quack like my silly old dad.
I want to be utterly other,
  And frightfully modern and mad.'

'Do you know,' said the turkey, 'you're quacking!
  There's a fox creeping up thro' the rye:
And if you're not utterly lacking,
  You'll make for that duck-pond. Good-bye!'

But the duckling was perky as perky.
  'Take care of your stuffing!' he called.
(This was horribly rude to a turkey!)
  'But you aren't a real turkey,' he bawled.

'You're an early Victorian sparrow!
  A fox is more fun than a sheep!
I shall show that my mind is not narrow
  And give him my feathers — to keep.'

Now the curious end of this fable,
  So far as the rest ascertained,
Though they searched from the barn to the stable,
  Was that only his feathers remained.

So he wasn't the bond-slave of habit,
  And he didn't have webs on his toes;
And perhaps he runs round like a rabbit,
  A rabbit as red as a rose.

Alfred Noyes

Hymns: *1* All things which live below the sky
2 Daisies are our silver, buttercups our gold

Prayer: For this new day — we thank you Father God.
Help us to use it well in every way.   *Amen*

31   The blind men and the Elephant

Perhaps you first learned about elephants from pictures of them. Possibly you met a real one at a circus, or even had a ride on one of these great creatures at the zoo. Here is a story of six blind men who wanted to learn about elephants.

The blind men and the Elephant
It was six men of Hindostan,
  To learning much inclined
Who went to see the Elephant,
  (Though all of them were blind);
That each by observation
  Might satisfy his mind.

57

The first approached the Elephant,
  And happening to fall
Against his broad and sturdy side,
  At once began to bawl:
'Bless me, it seems the Elephant
  Is very like a wall.'

The second, feeling of his tusk,
  Cried, 'Ho! what have we here
So very round and smooth and sharp?
  To me 'tis mighty clear
This wonder of an Elephant
  Is very like a spear.'

The third approached the animal,
  And happening to take
The squirming trunk within his hands,
  Then boldly up and spake:
'I see,' quoth he, 'the Elephant
  Is very like a snake.'

The fourth stretched out his eager hand
  And felt about the knee,
'What most this mighty beast is like
  Is mighty plain,' quoth he;
''Tis clear enough the Elephant
  Is very like a tree.'

The fifth who chanced to touch the ear
  Said, 'Even the blindest man
Can tell what this resembles most;
  Deny the fact who can,
This marvel of an Elephant
  Is very like a fan.'

The sixth no sooner had begun
  About the beast to grope,
Than, seizing on the swinging tail
  That fell within his scope,
'I see,' cried he, 'the Elephant
  Is very like a rope.'

And so these men of Hindostan
  Disputed loud and long,
Each in his own opinion
  Exceeding stiff and strong,
Though each was partly in the right
  And all were in the wrong.

John Godfrey Saxe

Hymns: *1* He gave me eyes so I could see
2 All things bright and beautiful

Prayer: To help us in our learning you give us eyes to see, ears to hear and hands to touch. Thank you Father God for all your gifts to us. *Amen*

32   Busy hands

A farmer's life is a busy one, whatever the type of farm. Some have acres of land, other are small-holdings — more like big gardens. Then there are some rather special farms, and our story begins on one of those.

It's quite small — about twenty acres — near the seaside town of Ramsgate in Kent. There's a herd of twelve Jersey cows as well as geese, hens and sheep. All the animals must be fed each day, the cows must be milked twice a day, and the milk prepared for sale to the Milk Marketing Board. Eggs must be collected, and the land must be cultivated. The soil on this farm is rich and fertile, producing fine vegetables for the farm workers and visitors to the small guest house, as well as food for the animals. You can see that the workers must be busy!

The special thing about this farm is that it is worked by fourteen nuns. Their home is not an ordinary farmhouse, but Minster Abbey. Like the farm, the Abbey is not very big. The Saxon wing is nearly one thousand years old and the nuns who work there have come from six different countries. Together they farm the land, look after the sheep and cows, and feed the geese and hens.

On the farm is an old stable and inside its heavy grey doors are six stalls where horses were kept years ago, when the Abbey was used as a private home. Close by is the room where the groom lived, and the fittings on the walls show where saddles and harnesses used to hang, in the days of horse-drawn carriages.

These days things are very different. The farm tractor now stands in the coach-house, and Sister Concordia, one of the nuns, has her workshop in the stable. Many years ago, before coming to Minster Abbey, Sister Concordia trained as a sculptor. So she was asked to make a bronze statue of Mary and Jesus, and for many months she went to the stable whenever she could to complete her task. When at last the statue was finished it was taken to Canterbury Cathedral.

Original pencil drawing for *Our Lady of Canterbury* statue, reproduced by permission of Sister Concordia Scott, OSB, of Minster Abbey.

Sister Concordia was one of the hundreds of people who went to Canterbury to listen to the Pope when he visited Britain in 1982. How happy she must have been to know that her statue of Mary and Jesus, the Madonna and Child, had been finished in time for the special day when the Pope visited the Cathedral.

Poems: *Down on the farm*
What a busy life to lead
 Cows to milk
 Hens to feed
 Sheep to count
 The geese might stray
 See no creature runs away.
Land to plough and crops to grow
God give us time our thanks to show.

What shall I make today?
Just a lump of clay
 My teacher gave to me today
A bird, a dragon or a fish?
 Perhaps I'll make a little dish.

Just a lump of clay
 My teacher gave to me today
But if I shape it carefully
 I'll make a figure just like me.

Hymns: *1* The farmer comes to scatter the seed
2 I have seen the golden sunshine
3 Golden cockerel

Prayer: Dear Lord, we have such busy hands. So much to learn, so much to do; may we be thoughtful and helpful too. *Amen*

Minster Abbey In AD 670, Domneva, grand-daughter of King Ethelbert (first Christian king of Kent) was given ground in Thanet to build a monastery for Benedictine nuns. This was in reparation for the murder of her two brothers by their cousin, who wanted to keep Kent for his own line. Her daughter Mildred succeeded her as Abbess and became a much-loved early Saxon saint. In the ninth century the Vikings burned down the Abbey. In 1027 monks of St Augustine built a manor house and farmed the land for 500 years. Following the dissolution of monasteries in the sixteenth century the house was sold privately. In 1936 a German Abbess from Bavaria bought the Abbey as a house of refuge from the Nazis, and now again — after 1100 years — Benedictine nuns are at Minster Abbey.

33 David and Goliath

When Saul was King of Israel, a great warrior of the Philistine army was troubling his country. The warrior's name was Goliath. He was nearly three metres tall and with all his armour on he looked a giant of a man. Each day the Israelite army and the Philistine army lined up on opposite hillsides. Between them lay the Valley of Elah.

Every morning Goliath put on his bronze helmet and the heavy armour that covered his body and legs. He slung a javelin over his shoulder and carried a huge spear tipped with bronze. Then, with a soldier walking in front of him to carry his shield, he shouted to the Israelites, 'What are you doing there lined up for battle? I am a Philistine, you slaves of Saul. Choose one of your men to fight me. If he wins and kills me, we will be your slaves; but if I win and kill him, you will be our slaves. Here and now I challenge the Israelite army. I dare you to pick someone to fight me.'

When Saul and his men heard this they were terrified. For forty days, every morning and evening, Goliath came out to threaten and dare the soldiers of the Israelite army.

At this time there lived in Bethlehem an old man called Jesse. He had eight sons. The three eldest were soldiers in Saul's army and the youngest boy, David, had the job of looking after his father's sheep.

One day Jesse said to David, 'I want you to go and find out how your brothers are. Take with you ten loaves of bread and some roasted grain, and I'll give you ten cheeses to take to the commanding officer. I want to know that you saw your brothers and whether they are well. There is trouble between the Israelite army and the Philistines in the Valley of Elah.'

David got up very early the next morning. He left someone in charge of the sheep and took the food as his father had told him. He arrived just as the two armies were taking their places on the hillsides. David left the food with the officer in charge and ran to his brothers to see how they were getting on. As they were talking together, Goliath came forward shouting to the Israelites as usual. When the Israelites saw Goliath they ran away in terror.

'Just look at the size of the man!' they shouted. 'Listen to his challenge! The king has promised a big reward to anyone who kills him. He's even said he will give his daughter, and stop all taxes on the family of such a man!'

David listened carefully and started asking the soldiers questions about Goliath. 'Who is this Philistine who dares to defy the army of the living God?' he asked.

This made his brothers angry. 'What are you doing here? You should be with your sheep. You cheeky brat, you only came here to watch the fighting!'

'Now what have I done?' David said. 'Can't I even ask a question?'

The soldiers had told King Saul about David and he sent for him.

'Your Majesty, no one should be afraid of this Philistine. I will go and fight him,' David began. The king replied, 'How could you fight him? You're just a boy, and he has been a soldier all his life.'

'Your Majesty,' said David, 'I take care of my father's sheep. When a lion or a bear carries off a lamb I go after it and rescue the lamb. If a lion or a bear turns on me I grab it by the throat. I have killed lions and bears and I will do the same to this Philistine. The Lord has saved me from wild animals; he will save me from this giant.'

'All right,' Saul answered. 'Go, and the Lord be with you.'

He gave his own armour to David, but when he strapped on the heavy coat, David found he couldn't walk.

'I can't fight in all this,' he said to the king. 'I'm not used to it.' So he took it all off and picked up his shepherd's stick. Then he chose five smooth stones from the stream, put them in his bag, and with his catapult ready he went out to meet Goliath.

The Philistine came towards David with his shield-bearer walking in front of him. When he was close enough to see David clearly he was angry to find such a young boy.

'What's the stick for, do you think I'm a dog?' he shouted. 'Come on, I'll give your body to the birds and animals to eat.'

David answered, 'You are coming against me with sword, spear and javelin and I come against you in the name of the Lord, the God of the Israelites. This day everyone will see that the Lord does not need swords and spears to save his people.'

Goliath started towards David again, but David took a stone from his bag and loaded his catapult. With careful and steady aim he slung the stone at Goliath. It hit him on the forehead and Goliath fell face down on the ground. Then David ran up, took Goliath's sword from its sheath, and killed him with it. When the Philistines saw that their warrior was dead, they turned and ran.

King Saul and his fighting men looked at David in amazement. He was their hero that day.

Hymns: *1* When a knight won his spurs in the stories of old
2 God be in my head and in my understanding

Prayer: From an ancient blessing for the people of Israel

Numbers 6.24–26

May the Lord bless you and take care of you;
May the Lord be kind and generous to you;
May the Lord give you peace. *Amen*

---

34 Springtime — fun time

Krishna was seven years old when he moved to Brindavan with his parents — Nanda the chief herdsman and his wife Yashoda. The rich green fields of Brindavan stretched far and wide, and many families settled happily there in huts which the men had built.

Very early each morning the herdsmen took their cattle out to graze in the lush fields. One day Krishna asked, 'Mother, please let me go with them. I'm a big boy now and I promise to look after myself.'

Yashoda smiled. Her son was growing up and she found it hard to refuse him, so after thinking for a moment, she agreed.

Krishna was so excited. 'Mother, can you give me a flute to take with me? One of the other boys has a flute and he plays such soft notes on it.'

'But Krishna, you don't know how to play a flute,' Yashoda said. 'Who will teach you?'

'Nobody — I'll teach myself,' was the confident reply.

So early the next morning Krishna took his flute and went with the cowherds into the fields with their cattle. He sat under a tree and began to blow on the instrument. The noises he made at first were very strange indeed, not a bit like music. But gradually he found the notes he wanted and learned to play soft and beautiful melodies. This really was music. The birds stopped their singing, and even the cows stood up to listen. Those who heard him said his music became more sweet each day. His friends noticed that when he played, everyone around him became more peaceful.

The years passed. Krishna became expert at looking after the cattle, and they grew to love him. The other boys were his friends, and the girls from the village would stop their work and run to the fields to listen when they heard his flute playing.

Krishna had always been a mischievous boy and he liked playing tricks on his friends. He never hurt anyone, but loved to have fun and tease them.

Each spring a Festival of Colours was held. This gave Krishna an idea. 'Let's collect some buckets and fill them with water,' he said to his friends. So early in the morning the boys carried buckets of water to the fields. They hid them behind trees near the grazing ground and Krishna sprinkled coloured powder into each one. Then they all went to sit by the cattle. The cowherds settled down quietly as usual, and Krishna, leaning against a tree, began to play his flute. The sound of his music floated on the breeze until it reached the village.

In a few minutes the village girls, dressed in their new clothes for the festival, came out into the fields. Krishna pretended to be playing with his eyes closed until they were very near, then he called to his friends. The girls squealed with laughter as they were showered with coloured water! Although they pretended to be cross at their soaking, everyone enjoyed the fun.

As he grew older, Krishna still enjoyed teasing his friends — especially girls! Every morning the milkmaids would get up early and go for a swim in the river Yamuna before they went to work. One day, while the girls were enjoying their swim, Krishna crept to the place where they had laid their clothes and very quietly gathered them up. Then he climbed a tree and hid in its leafy branches. When the swimmers came out of the water, of course they couldn't find their clothes. As they searched they heard soft music, and straight away recognised the magic tones of Krishna's flute. They looked into the tree and there he was, with their clothes hanging all round him!

'We should have known it would be Krishna,' said one girl.

'Hark at him still playing his flute and us without our clothes!' exclaimed another girl.

They all called out, 'Hurry up, Krishna! Throw down our things!'

At last, with a laugh, he gave them back their clothes. Then off he went — probably planning what his next prank would be!

A Hindu prayer
I pray not for wealth,
I pray not for honours,
I pray not for pleasures,
   nor even the joys of poetry.
I only pray that through all my life
   I may have love.
            Chaitanya, AD 1500

Hymns: *1* The golden cockerel
2 I love the sun

Prayer: Father God, we thank you for the joy of springtime; for the spring flowers and blossom on the trees. We thank you for the happy days we share together.   *Amen*

The most important gods of contemporary Hinduism are Vishnu and Siva. Vishnu is benevolent and supreme and reappears on earth in successive incarnations or avatars. The most popular of the avatars of Vishnu is Krishna, god of love.

---

35   The man who looked like Father Christmas

It was half term holiday. Jane Biggs and her brother Tom had just finished breakfast, and Tom was planning to play football with his friends. Jane, however, was glad she was old enough to go with her father to the garage where he worked.

As they neared the garage Jane asked, 'Do you think the road sweeper will call today, Dad? He always looks like Father Christmas to me!'

'Perhaps he will,' her dad replied. 'Mr Vaughan is a cheerful old man, and I'm always pleased to see him.'

Business was brisk at the garage that morning. There was the usual queue of cars waiting to use the petrol pumps, and several drivers called into the shop, where Jane helped to serve them. Later she brought a mug of hot coffee to her dad as he checked the petrol records.

'Here comes Mr Vaughan now, Jane. With this cold wind today I'm sure he would like a hot drink too.'

It had become a habit for Bill Vaughan to call in at the garage. He always bought a packet of mints from the shop and enjoyed a friendly chat with Mr Biggs when he wasn't busy.

'That's mighty kind of you, Miss Jane,' he thanked her. As he stood sipping the hot coffee Jane looked at the bushy white beard, the ruddy face and the old hat with feathers tucked in the band. She knew many people laughed at him and some were even a little afraid of this old man, with his long grey coat and hob-nailed boots. As usual he didn't stay long.

'Good morning to you both, I must be on my way. Thanks again for the coffee.' He disappeared round the corner, pushing the cart that carried the broom and tools he used for cleaning the kerbs and pavements.

Eventually Bill Vaughan retired from road sweeping, but he would call in at the garage from time to time to buy his mints and see Mr Biggs. He still wore the same grey coat and feathered hat.

One morning, seeing him arrive, Mr Biggs called out, 'Morning, Bill. Why so glum today? It's not like you!'

He sighed, 'I have to leave the rooms where I'm living as the house is to be sold. No one else seems to be able to help. Perhaps you know of someone with a room to let?'

Mr Biggs promised to think about it and that evening he told his family about the problem Bill Vaughan was having in finding a place to live.

Olive, his wife, said, 'We have a spare room and I'd be happy for him to come here if the rest of the family agree.' After talking it over it was agreed that Mr Vaughan would be invited to join the Biggs family in their home.

It didn't take long for Bill Vaughan to settle in. He brought a battered suitcase that contained his clothes and two old watches that sometimes worked. He enjoyed Mrs Biggs' good cooking and the family chatter at mealtimes. In the evenings he disappeared to his room, but off he would go early every morning to a small piece of land about a mile away, where he cared for two geese and a few hens. Some days he would proudly place a few brown eggs on the kitchen table, saying, 'There you are, Mrs Biggs, nothing like a really fresh egg for breakfast.'

A few years passed in this way. Bill Vaughan lived happily with the Biggs family and they became very fond of him. Then one day old Bill died. He left all he had to his friends who had given him a home. The battered suitcase, the two watches that sometimes worked and the land with two geese and a few hens on it. When a builder wanted to buy the land for new houses, Mr Biggs was surprised to learn that it was worth a great deal of money — £76,000!

Whenever he was asked why they had given a home to old Bill when everyone else refused, Mr Biggs would say, 'He just needed help. We didn't agree he looked like a tramp. To us he looked like Father Christmas.'

Poem: *A feather for my cap*
Seagull flying from the sea,
   Drop a feather here for me!
Drop it down into my lap
   I need a feather for my cap.
I. O. Eastwick

Hymns: *1* When I needed a neighbour were you there?
2 God who made the earth
3 All things bright and beautiful

Prayer: Dear Father God, we remember the people who help us
by their work. May our hands be busy and helpful today.   *Amen*

---

36   Mr John's new friend

Nurse Joyce pushed open the door of the small ward where Mr John
and his son were sitting. The sun shone through the window and
made the daffodils in the vase on the table shine like gold.

'Well now, Mr John, it's good for you to have your son to see you
today!' Although she gave her big cheery smile only the visitor smiled
back. Mr John was an old man and had been very ill for some time.
Often he was rather bad-tempered and grumpy and today he was
even worse.

'I was just saying that nothing in here seems to be working properly today. It's been noisy all morning. I feel too hot, even though
my dinner was half cold when it arrived. It's all because of you
darkies! You and your sort cause all the trouble.'

The old man's son looked most uncomfortable. 'I'm sorry Nurse,
my father isn't feeling well and . . .'

Nurse Joyce stopped him quietly. 'Now, there's no need to make
excuses for him. I'm going to help someone else for a while.'

Outside the room the nurse sighed. She felt cross and upset, and
thought to herself, 'Why should I take that from him? Why should
I?' She carried on down the long hospital corridor thinking deeply
as she went. 'Why should I? Why should I?' Suddenly she stopped,
remembering . . . of course . . . she had to go back and help him.

Turning round she hurried back to the little room to find the old
man slumped in his chair, all alone. 'Come along then, Mr John, let
me help you.'

For the next half hour she worked, bringing water to bathe his face
and hands, making the bed comfortable and helping him back into
it. Then she put cream on the sore places of his arms and legs and
gently powdered them. When he was settled, she moved the vase of
flowers closer and put his favourite magazine within reach. Finally,
she turned the photographs of his young grandchildren towards the
bed, in the hope that their laughing faces might cheer him up. As
she moved to the door at last, he spoke to her. 'Nurse.'

'What is it, Mr John?' she replied. 'I've done all I can for you to make you comfortable and happy. Tell me if I can do any more and I will.'

The old man almost whispered his reply. 'Nurse Joyce, please pray for me.'

Quietly the nurse pulled the small blind over the window to the corridor and walked back to the bed. She put her strong arms round the old man and prayed.

'Dear God, please bless Mr John and make him happy and well. I thank you Lord for reminding me that Jesus loves us and we must love each other; we remember for Jesus' sake. Amen.'

The room seemed very quiet and peaceful as she finished the short prayer. Mr John smiled for the first time that day.

'Thank you Nurse, you don't know how good that makes me feel. I'm so glad we're friends now.'

The next week the young man again came to visit his father, who had been moved into a different ward. Another visitor came to see Mr John that day too. It was Nurse Joyce, and she had brought him a big bunch of spring flowers. The old man put his arms round her and gave her a kiss.

'Hallo, my dear. I'm so pleased to see you.'

In surprise, his son laughed. 'And I'm pleased to see you too. Thank you for making my father so happy!'

Poem: *Caring for others*

When your heart is light
  And the day is fair
Do you ever suddenly
  Stop and care?

Care what is happening
  To the others
Who after all
  Are sisters and brothers?

Does it ever strike you,
  I'm happy and free,
And I wish all people
  Could be like me?

If you're lucky and safe
  Could you sometimes say,
'Please, God, let nothing
  Be hurt today.'

Anon.

Hymns: *1* When I needed a neighbour were you there?
2 All things bright and beautiful

Prayer: Dear God, we remember that Jesus loves us. Please help us to love each other. *Amen*

The words Nurse Joyce remembered were: 'If your enemy is hungry feed him; if he is thirsty, give him a drink . . . do not let evil conquer you, but use good to defeat evil.' *Romans 12.20–21*

37 Krishna and Sudama

Krishna was growing into a fine lad. His father, the king, was proud of him, but he knew that as Krishna was a prince he would need to study the Vedas (Hindu Holy Books) and learn how to use weapons. He decided to send him to the ashram of Sandipani. This ashram was a large but simple hermitage, or home, and Sandipani was thought to be the wisest and best teacher of that time. He had many pupils — some were the sons of kings, like Krishna; others were the sons of poor Brahmin priests. He treated all the boys the same. They swept and cleaned the rooms, they chopped wood and gathered wild fruits from the forest. Krishna did the work happily and in class he listened carefully to the wise words of his teacher. Sandipani was very pleased with him.

One day a boy called Sudama joined the ashram. He was the son of a Brahmin priest, a quiet and gentle boy, and Krishna liked him straight away. The two boys became friends, and as they worked together they grew to love each other like brothers.

When chopping wood in the forest one morning Sudama said, 'Krishna, we will leave here when our studies are finished. You will become a king and live in a palace, and I shall be a teacher. I expect I shall be as poor as my father. Will you remember me?'

'What a thing to say!' Krishna replied. 'How does being poor or rich make a difference to friends? I shall always love you like a brother.'

Sudama smiled a little sadly and wondered if Krishna really would remember him. 'Please play your flute, Krishna,' he asked, 'and then tell me again about your adventures in Brindavan.'

Krishna put the flute to his lips and soon the forest rang with sweet music. Not long after this, Krishna's father died, so he had to leave the ashram and say goodbye to his friend Sudama.

On his return home, he found that the people were being threatened by another king's armies, so he stayed to help them. He became a great soldier and led his people in many adventures. In time he brought them to the western seashore of the country, where they built the wonderful city of Dwarka. Everyone was free to live there in peace, away from the danger of the enemy. A palace was built for Krishna and he married the beautiful Princess Rukmini. Through all his adventures, even as king, Krishna often thought about his boyhood friends, especially Sudama.

Meanwhile, life had been very different for Sudama. After leaving the ashram he did become a teacher. He had a good wife and a lovely little girl, but he was sad because they were so poor. He didn't mind his own clothes being ragged, but he hated to see his daughter in torn clothes and sometimes crying with hunger.

At last his wife said to him, 'Sudama, you are always telling us about your friend Krishna. I hear he is a great king now. Surely if you go to him and tell him how poor we are, he will want to help.'

'Perhaps he won't remember me,' thought Sudama. He didn't like to ask his old friend for help, but when he looked at his little girl he agreed to go.

It was a long way to travel and the journey made him very tired. At the palace a servant went to Krishna and said, 'There's a poor Brahmin at the door. He won't go away. He keeps saying that he is Sudama and he wishes to see you!'

Krishna jumped to his feet. He ran as quickly as he could through the long corridors of the palace until he found his friend. Oh, how tired and ill he looked! Krishna led Sudama to a bed and, taking a bowl of water, gently bathed his dusty, blistered feet. The servants were told to prepare food, and soon the two friends were talking together as they had done so many years ago.

'Which village do you live in?' Krishna asked. Sudama told him where it was. Later, when Sudama fell asleep, Krishna told his servants to go to the village and build a fine house.

'Fill it with money, food and clothes,' he ordered. 'You must make sure that Sudama and his family have everything they need.'

The friends spent several happy days together but Sudama didn't like to ask Krishna for help, and Krishna didn't ask if he needed anything. When the time came for Sudama to leave, a chariot was ordered to take him back to his village. As Krishna waved goodbye to his friend he couldn't help smiling as he thought of the wonderful surprise Sudama would find when he reached home.

A Hindu prayer
You are my mother, and you are my father.
You are my friend, and you are my teacher.
You are my wisdom, and you are my riches.
You are everything to me, O God of all Gods.
Ramanuja, AD 1100

Saying: A friend in need is a friend indeed!

Hymns: *1* Praise him, praise him
2 The family of man
3 He gave me eyes so I could see

Prayer: Father God, we remember the people we love and those who love us. Especially we thank you for our friends. *Amen*

38 A sign of love

You can't help noticing all the bright lights when you walk around a town or city after dark. There are street-lights; lights from cars; lights from shops and offices; brightly-coloured neon lights flashing advertisements, all making you look and wonder, just like the creatures in this story who saw a rainbow light up the sky.

From *History of the Flood*

Bang Bang Bang
Said the nails in the Ark.

It's getting rather dark
Said the nails in the Ark.

For the rain is coming down
Said the nails in the Ark.

And you're all like to drown
Said the nails in the Ark.

Dark and black as sin
Said the nails in the Ark.

So won't you all come in
Said the nails in the Ark.

But only two by two
Said the nails in the Ark.

So they came in two by two
The elephant, the kangaroo,
And the gnu,
And the little tiny shrew.

Then the birds
Flocked in like winged words:
Two racket-tailed motmots, two macaws,
Two nuthatches and two
Little bright robins.

And the reptiles: the gila monster, the slow-worm,
The green mamba, the cotton mouth, and the alligator —
All squirmed in;
And after a very lengthy walk,
Two giant Galapagos tortoises.

And the insects in their hierarchies;
A queen ant, a king ant, a queen wasp, a king wasp,
A queen bee, a king bee,
And all the beetles, bugs and mosquitoes,
Cascaded in like glittering, murmurous jewels . . .

God put a rainbow in the sky.
They wondered what it was for.
There had never been a rainbow before.
The rainbow was a sign;
It looked like a neon sign —
Seven colours arched in the skies:
What should it publicise?
They looked up with wondering eyes.

It advertises Mercy
Said the nails in the Ark.

Mercy, Mercy, Mercy
Said the nails in the Ark.

Our God is merciful
Said the nails in the Ark.

Merciful and gracious
Bang Bang Bang Bang.

John Heath Stubbs

Saying: The sign of love — Jesus said at the crucifixion:
'Forgive them Father, they don't know what they are doing.'

Luke 23.34

Hymns: *1* I'm very glad of God
2 Jesus, friend of little children

Prayer: Dear Father God, we thank you for all your love and kindness to us. Help us to be kind and loving in all we think and in all we do today, for Jesus' sake.   *Amen*

---

39 The promise

When a king is crowned he promises to care for his people as well as he can. After delicious meals at home you may promise to help with the washing up. Making a promise is a very serious thing, and our story is about a village whose people made a promise to God.

Choir, 1980 Passion Play.　*Photograph:* © *Gemeinde Oberammergau*

Crucifixion, 1980 Passion Play.　*Photograph:* © *Gemeinde Oberammergau*

Hundreds of years ago, the people of a beautiful mountain village called Oberammergau, in the Ammer Valley of Bavaria, were troubled with war. The army of King Gustave Adolf of Sweden had attacked the village and before the soldiers left they set fire to houses, the church and even the crops in the fields, leaving the people hungry and frightened. Nearby villages also suffered as wandering bands of soldiers attacked the people, stole food, and, worst of all, they left behind a terrible illness called the plague. Almost everyone who caught this illness died. In Oberammergau the people tried hard to protect themselves by building great fires around the village and setting watchmen to make sure that no strangers entered.

One day a man called Kaspar Schisler decided that he would like to visit his family in nearby Oberammergau to enjoy a special feast day with them. Having heard about the watchmen and their bonfires, Kaspar knew they would never let him through, so he climbed the mountain paths and managed to slip into his old home on the edge of the village without the guards noticing him. But Kaspar didn't know he was carrying the plague, and within two days he died of it. It spread like wildfire, and the following year many families died of the illness, causing great sadness in Oberammergau.

The Village Council held an emergency meeting and racked their brains to think of something they could do to help their people. They decided to meet in the church next day and there they made a solemn promise to God. They promised to perform a Passion Play every ten years, to tell the story of Jesus, the way he suffered and was killed and the way he came back to life again. They made this vow, praying that God would have mercy on them and free them from the plague. From that day, the 27th of October 1634, no one else in the village of Oberammergau died of plague.

The villagers acted their first Passion Play in the church where they made the promise. Since then they have kept their promise to God and regularly perform the story of Jesus Christ. Through the years the words have changed and the songs and music have been rewritten, but the story is the same.

In time the play became famous and a stage had to be built in the churchyard, so that more people could take part. Now, when the villagers act their Passion Play, thousands of people travel from all over the world to see it. For the thirty-seventh performance in 1980 there were 676 boys and girls taking part, between the ages of seven and seventeen. They were divided into four groups and took turns to act on different days — alongside their parents and grandparents, in some cases!

Young children of three and four years also go on the stage with their parents. They all look forward to the year when it will be their turn to act in the story of Jesus for the first time. As they grow older they take different parts. It is of course a great honour for a man to be chosen to play the part of Jesus, or for a woman to be Mary his mother.

The last play took nine months to prepare, and the children involved were given special permission for a long summer holiday and time off school for the performance, but all the lost lessons had to be made up!

When summer is over and the thousands of visitors have gone, the people of Oberammergau go back to their ordinary lives. Once again the promise made by their ancestors hundreds of years ago has been kept, and they have told the world the message of peace to all nations in the name of Jesus.

Poem:　　Children in the village school of Shalfleet, Isle of Wight, were thinking about the story of Jesus and wrote this poem.

Now upon a mountain,
Jesus and his friends,
Gather for the last time
As his time ends.
As he stands there talking,
With a smile upon his face,
He slowly rises from the earth,
And ascends up into space.

As they stand there gazing,
Up into the sky,
A cloud came down and hid him,
Then two angels caught their eye.
Why look up into Heaven,
For he will come again,
He'll always be here with us,
Through life, love and pain.

Hymns:　　*1* Jesus, friend of little children
2 Jesus' hands were kind hands

Prayer:　　Dear God, we remember the promise of Jesus to his friends: 'I am with you always.' When we make a promise, may we be careful to keep our word.　*Amen*

---

40 Easter treasure

Sometimes treasure is found by accident. Many farmers ploughing their fields have found a hoard of coins that has been hidden in the ground for years. Some people spend a long time searching for treasure and sometimes they get a surprise.

Professor Richmond was like this. He taught his students at Oxford about the Roman Empire. He knew that at Inchtuthil, near

Perth in Scotland, the Romans had built a fortress nearly two thousand years ago. Although all the buildings had gone and there was nothing to be seen on the ground, the Professor and his friends began digging. They soon found trenches where the walls had been, and slowly they uncovered the shape and plan of the fortress — the barracks where Roman soldiers had lived, officers' houses, the hospital, and where great workshops had once been. This was where the Roman wagons must have come to be mended. For nine years the Professor and his friends gradually explored the old fortress site that had once been a camp for more than five thousand Roman soldiers.

The soldiers had been at Inchtuthil for six years when they were given an order:

'You must leave at once. The Roman army is in trouble in the south. Bring all you can carry and destroy everything else!'

The soldiers made a good job of the destruction. All the buildings were burned down, every pot in the pottery was broken into small pieces, even the drains were filled. No one could use the fortress after they left.

One day the Professor noticed that the soil in the trench he was exploring was darker than usual. He dug deeper, and revealed ten iron wheel tyres and below that a crusted mass of iron. Hundreds of iron nails had rusted together like a sheet. Digging even deeper, the Professor could hardly believe his eyes. He had found his treasure. Thousands more iron nails were under the top blanket of nails. Some were a little rusty — others shone almost like new!

In time all the nails were dug out. There were over three-quarters of a million nails, in four sizes from five centimetres to forty centimetres long. They weighed seven tonnes altogether, and filled more than a hundred crates. Each nail had been hammered to a spike shape, with a solid flat head.

The news of Professor Richmond's treasure spread. Thousands of nails were sold for twenty-five pence each, to pay for the cost of the dig. In Scotland the nails were used to make a cross for a church. People from all over the world wanted to buy them. For some it was because they wanted to own something as old as that.

For other people the nails meant something else. Around the same time as the soldiers at Inchtuthil buried their nails, other Roman soldiers had a job to do, nearer home. They were given a handful of nails to make three crosses.

It was nails like these that caused the terrible scars on the hands of Jesus which his friends saw when they met him on the very first Easter.

Poem: *Easter treasure*
                  Men seek for treasure in the ground
                    And golden coins some have found.
                  God's treasure for the world to find
                    The love of Jesus for mankind.

Hymns: *1* Daisies are our silver, buttercups our gold
2 I danced in the morning
3 God has given us a book full of stories

Prayer: Day by day,
              Dear Lord, of thee three things I pray:
              To see thee more clearly,
              Love thee more dearly,
              Follow thee more nearly,
              Day by day.
                              St Richard of Chichester (c.1197–1253)

The fortress at Inchtuthil, built in AD 83, was the advance headquarters of Agricola, the Roman general and governor of Britain who advanced Roman rule north to the Firth of Forth.

41 To greet the summer term

The autumn and spring terms are gone. Another term has just begun — the last term of our school year!

School fanfare
Sound the trumpets, beat the drums,
Another term has just begun.

Mother has bought the uniform,
Peter has been to the barber,
Dinner money is back in the purse,
Now for some peace says father.

The school is ready to start anew,
The floor in the hall is gleaming.
The caretaker's peace is over once more
In the staff room the kettle is steaming.

It's back to the work on the reading scheme,
The joy of new books and best writing;
Arithmetic and modern maths,
Work hard, play well, no fighting!

So sound the trumpet and beat the drum,
Another term has just begun.

There are times when most of us wish we were a little cleverer. Have you ever thought that it would be so good to be first for a change, instead of always last or in the middle? If you have, you'll be interested in the tale of the hare and the tortoise.

Mr Hare and Mr Tortoise met one day and agreed to have a race, the following Saturday at one o'clock. All their friends decided that they would come to watch the great event, and cheer on their favourite.

When the race started, Mr Hare ran off as fast as his strong legs would carry him. Of course Mr Tortoise, with his short stumpy legs, moved much more slowly. Soon all he could see of Mr Hare was a puff of dust in the distance. But the race track was long, and Mr Tortoise kept on doing his best, just plod, plod, plodding on.

When Mr Hare had almost reached the end of the track he saw a field of juicy-looking carrots. He looked around. There was no sign of Mr Tortoise! He had plenty of time for a good chew — the running had made him so hungry. When Mr Hare had eaten his fill there was still no sign of Mr Tortoise, so he decided there was time for a short nap before running on to win the race.

As he slept, Mr Tortoise came plodding along. He plodded as quietly as he could past the sleeping Mr Hare, right past the finishing post, to his own surprise and to the delight of his friends. How they all cheered! The noise woke up Mr Hare, who realised that he had lost the race.

Remember that it isn't always the one who makes the quickest start who does best in the end.

Bible reference: I am certain that nothing can separate us from his love . . . there is nothing in all creation that will ever be able to separate us from the love of God . . .   *Romans* 8.28–29

Hymns: *1* The sun that shines across the sea
2 Father hear the prayer we offer

Prayer: Another term — another day,
              Help us, dear God, in every way,
              To do our very best today. *Amen*

42 The wanderer

About ten o'clock one morning Mr Lowdon looked out of his front window to see what all the commotion was about. The traffic had stopped, drivers were hooting their horns, and passers-by were shouting and waving their arms. Whatever was wrong? He looked up and down the street. Then he saw the cause of the outcry — a big fat swan was waddling around in the middle of the narrow High Street!

Wanting to help, Mr Lowdon picked up a piece of bread from the kitchen and ran outside. Everyone seemed frightened of the big bird and people were trying to shoo him away. The more they shooed and shouted, the more the swan hissed at them and flapped strong angry wings.

'That's not the way to do it,' Mr Lowdon thought.

'Let me have a go with him,' he called out. 'Come on Charlie, come on now.' He coaxed the bird gently, holding out a piece of bread.

No one knows whether the swan's name really was Charlie, but he stopped hissing and eyed Mr Lowdon gravely.

'Come on Charlie, be a good boy!'

The bird hissed again and his wings began to lift, then slowly he relaxed and moved closer to the piece of bread.

The crowd watched in amazement as Mr Lowdon patiently coaxed the big bird into following him. Once the swan had been persuaded to leave the road, the traffic began to move again and everyone lost interest, but Mr Lowdon kept talking to Charlie and leading the bird towards his garden.

'There's a good Charlie,' he said, as the swan settled onto a bank of soft grass by the rockery. He arranged a piece of fencing to make a temporary pen, where Charlie seemed happy to rest.

'Now what do we do?' asked Mrs Lowdon. 'We can't keep a swan in the garden for long.'

'I'll telephone the police,' replied her husband. 'I expect they'll be able to help.'

The police told him to contact the RSPCA, who would know just what to do.

'We'll help you with pleasure,' said the man from the RSPCA, 'but we can't come until tomorrow morning.'

Mr Lowdon told his wife that Charlie would have to spend the night with them. They looked at the swan, and he seemed comfortable and quiet.

'I'll get some water for him,' said Mrs Lowdon, 'and you go across to the baker and see if he can spare some bread for our visitor.'

Charlie surprised his new friends by gulping down six pints of water. The baker kindly sent a bag of bread and buns, then a farmer friend brought a bale of straw. No wonder Charlie seemed happy as he settled down for the night.

Early the next morning, an RSPCA Inspector arrived in his small van. He gently examined Charlie's wings.

'One wing has been injured,' he explained. 'I'll be able to fix that and then I'll take him to the local pond. He should settle down with the other birds.'

The Lowdons waved goodbye to Charlie and the Inspector. The excitement was over and they had work to do.

After lunch they were surprised by a loud knocking at the front door. Their neighbour called in an excited voice, 'Bill, the swan is back in your garden!'

'He can't be!' thought Mr Lowdon, but sure enough, there was Charlie. It seemed as though the bird was looking at him with a friendly twinkle in his eye.

'Well, well,' said the RSPCA Inspector, when he was told the news on the van radio. 'I'll be right over to pick him up again.'

This time the Inspector took Charlie back to his own home. Resting in his garden was another injured swan, and the two birds seem to get on very well together. It was obviously no use setting Charlie free on the pond, as he would only wander into the High Street again, so the Inspector put both birds into his van and drove to the river a few miles away, where there was a small harbour. The Harbour Master gave permission for the swans to be released into the water.

The two men watched as the birds swam around for a while, then climbed out on to the bank. They couldn't help smiling as Charlie and his new mate waddled away, side by side, along the tow-path and out of sight.

Hymns: *1* All things which live below the sky
2 For the beauty of the earth

Prayer: Dear Father God, we thank you for all the creatures of this earth; for the birds that fly and fish that swim and for the animals both small and big. We remember the people who are helpful and kind to them. *Amen*

43　Two kinds of people

It is said that there are just two kinds of people in this world — the givers and the takers. People who give share what they have, and make life happier for everyone. But people who take don't bother about anybody but themselves. In these two short stories we see what can happen to them!

First there is the story of the vain sadhu — an Indian holy man — who went around telling everyone how good he was. Because of his saffron clothes and long beard, people knelt down and bowed to him. The more they bowed the more vain he became.

He visited a strange village one day and noticed a crowd watching two rams fighting. The sadhu sat down on a stone, hoping that everyone would see him. When nobody took any notice, he cleared his throat and gave a little cough. Still no one in the crowd noticed him, but one of the rams did. For some reason the ram didn't like the look of the sadhu, and decided to attack him. A ram has a habit of lowering its head before it charges. When this ram lowered its head, the vain sadhu thought that it was bowing in respect, and he felt very pleased with himself. The crowd saw what was about to happen and shouted to him to move away. Instead he raised his hand to bless the ram. The next moment the ram charged and knocked him flat on the ground. Perhaps that taught him a lesson!

The second story is about a greedy man who found himself in trouble. He was a young man who liked to explore the countryside and visit new places. In one village this lad met an old man from a poor family, who could neither read nor write, but he did know how to perform a miracle. Every day this old man would go into the forest, stand under a mango tree and utter a charm. The tree would immediately become heavy with ripe fruit, which would soon fall to the ground. The old man would collect the mangoes, eat some himself, then share the rest with his neighbours who were also poor.

The young man was so impressed and delighted that he fell to his knees and begged the old man to tell his secret charm. Reluctantly the old man agreed, but warned him, 'You must never use the spell to satisfy your greed. Also you must remember that the charm will only work if you do not tell a lie.'

When the young man returned to his own village he repeated the spell several times a day underneath the mango trees. Before long he had a large quantity of delicious fruit, which he sold in the market place. In a few months he became very rich.

When the king heard of this miracle he summoned the young man to his palace and asked, 'Where did you learn your spell?'

At first the lad was too proud to admit that he had learned it from a poor old man who could neither read nor write.

'Oh King,' he boasted, 'I learned it after much study under a group of great scholars in a far away University.'

'Well, perform a miracle for us now,' the king ordered.

The king, his family and a crowd of ministers followed the young man into the royal orchard. Under a big mango tree, the lad recited his charm. Nothing happened! He had told a lie, so the spell could not work.

Sadly the young man had to tell the truth to the king, who said, 'You have behaved badly to your teacher. If you go and apologise to him perhaps the charm will work again.'

So he found the poor old man again and apologised, but never again did the spell work, for he had used it just to satisfy greed. Perhaps that taught him a lesson, too!

The Nootka Indians of North America used this spell when they hoped for fair weather:

> You, whose day it is,
> Make it beautiful.
> Get out your rainbow colours
> So it will be beautiful.

Buddha once said: Three things cannot long be hidden,
The sun, the moon and the truth!

Hymns: *1* The sun that shines across the sea
2 To God who makes all lovely things

Prayer: May we try to follow this good advice: think kind thoughts; do things for a good reason; speak the truth; behave as well as possible; care for all living creatures; be as helpful as we can; not act without thinking; and always try our hardest.   *Amen*

The two stories are part of the 457 Jatakas, related by Gautama Siddhartha, the Buddha. Each of these tales contains a moral, and they reflect the experiences Buddha is said to have gained in previous incarnations. The prayer is an adaptation of the advice given in the Noble Eightfold Path, from the first sermon of the Buddha.

44 A new chair for David

This story starts in June 1981, when David's mother and father wanted to buy him a new chair. The chair had to be rather special because David is a rather special person. Not only was he born with deformed legs, feet, arms and hands, but he is a great sportsman. He needed an electric wheelchair, which would cost nearly £1000, but his parents couldn't afford this.

At school the headteacher suggested, 'Perhaps you would like to help raise some of the money, David? You could do a one-mile sponsored swim.' David thought this was a great idea.

Although David wasn't able to walk, he was determined to do as much as possible. He had learned to swim and could swim a mile by the time he was eight. David loved sports, especially swimming, javelin or discus throwing, and wheelchair racing. By the time he was fifteen, he had won many gold medals and cups. He had even won the school trophy for the most outstanding achievements in sport.

Everything was arranged for David to do a sponsored swim in the autumn, and his friends organised raffles, barbecues, jumble sales and discos to raise more money. But first, David and his mother and father planned a holiday in Spain. Every year they went to a small fishing village called Estartit, and met friends they had made over the years.

Two of David's friends, Pam and Ernie, wanted to help with the fund for his new wheelchair. They talked it over with another old friend, Tony, who owned a night club. The next time he saw David he said, 'I've got an idea. I'll help you raise the money for your wheelchair, if you'll swim the length of the harbour with me.'

With no hesitation David replied, 'Well, I've never swum in the sea before, but I'll have a go!'

During the next week Pam made posters to advertise David's swim; Tony auctioned bottles of champagne; and a well-known artist painted three portraits of David. He sold two and kept the other to auction after the swim. All the money went towards the chair-fund.

At three o'clock on the day of the swim a procession of about fifty people, led by David, set out from Tony's club. A friend who owned a laundry arrived with buckets to use as collecting boxes. As the parade moved along the sea front, holiday-makers sitting outside cafés and hotels left their tables to join in. By the time David was ready to swim, about three hundred people were standing watching from the shore. Many of them wanted to swim with David, but only twelve were allowed to go, provided they kept behind him.

The Harbour Commander arrived and moved boats that might have been in the way, then David was lifted into the water. He swam strongly to the end of the harbour wall, while the watching crowd cheered wildly at every stroke. The Harbour Commander, following in his launch, offered David a lift back to the beach. He was astounded to hear David shout, 'No thanks!' and signal that he wanted to swim back. The cheers from the shore crescendoed to a great roar, and when David arrived at the beach the noise was deafening.

'How do you feel, David?' asked his father, as he lifted him into the wheelchair.

'Great, I thoroughly enjoyed that,' was his son's reply.

Everyone came to congratulate him, and the laundry buckets were heavy with money given by the crowds who had watched David swim. His friend Tony had been collecting in a china-football money box. It was very precious to Tony because it had *Chelsea Football Club* written on it. Although David tried to stop him, he broke it in pieces to get the money out, saying, 'Here you are. You're worth it, mate!'

Three weeks after the family returned home, Pam sent a cheque for £525 — the money that had been collected! Together with their savings, at last there was enough to buy David's electric wheel-chair.

But that isn't the end of the story. David still swam his sponsored mile in the autumn, and with the help of money from events organised by his friends, there was more than £2000 in the fund.

David knew just how he wanted the money to be spent. Not only did he get a new chair, but he was also able to buy one for his friend Ian, as a wonderful surprise! The rest of the money bought new track-suits for the school sports team.

David and his parents will always remember the summer of the sponsored swims, and the help of so many friends.

Hymns: *1* Father hear the prayer we offer
2 I'm very glad of God

Prayer: Dear Father God, we pray —
      That you will help us all,
      To be brave, strong and kind today.   *Amen*

With David's deformities to arms and legs he is confined to a wheelchair. His first two years of life were spent in hospital, and since then he has attended hospital regularly for treatment, and received frequent manipula-tive surgery. Thanks to the efforts of his parents and the special school he attended, not to mention his own fighting determination, he has won many honours in sports, locally, nationally and internationally.

45 Lifeboat to the rescue!

Hayling is rather an unusual island. The north shore is linked to the Hampshire coast by a road bridge, while the sandy beaches to the south meet the busy Solent waters. The lifeboat station is there, on the south-east tip of the island.

One stormy December afternoon Frank Dunster noticed red flares in the sky, which meant that a boat was in danger at sea. Frank was a member of the lifeboat crew and knew what had to be done. He raced to the boathouse to help prepare the boat for its rescue work. The officer in charge could not be reached by telephone, so maroons were fired which exploded in the sky like noisy firework rockets. Almost immediately the Duty Launching Officer arrived.

The coastguard reported that the distress flares had come from *Fitz's Flyer*, a seven metre yacht with a broken rudder, impossible to control in the heavy seas. The force 8 gale could dash the yacht and its crew of four on to the shore. A Royal Navy helicopter had been sent out, but the seas were so rough that it couldn't get near enough to help.

There was no time to waste. The Duty Officer gave orders to launch the lifeboat immediately. Frank Dunster was to be the helmsman and two shore helpers, Trevor Pearce and Graham Wickham, had to crew, as there was no time to wait for anyone else to turn up. Frank tuned the two powerful engines to almost full speed as the boat ploughed into waves almost two metres high.

Over the bar of Chichester Harbour, the waves were even more frightening. The lifeboat was tossed in the air and the engines stalled as it crashed down into a trough between giant waves. Frank re-started the engines and made sure his crew were safe. As they lashed up the ropes that had been swept loose, he steered towards the helicopter hovering near the stricken yacht. Through the rain and spray he saw the shape of *Fitz's Flyer*. The crew had managed to drop anchor, and Frank tried to bring the lifeboat alongside.

At the first attempt another giant wave broke over them, and again the engines stopped. Frank only just managed to restart them in time to avoid a collision. The second time the sea tossed the lifeboat aside, but on the third run the crew managed to grab two men from the yacht. The next man to be rescued had an artificial leg and was more difficult to help. It took another four runs before he could jump onto the lifeboat. At last he made it, but landed heavily on Trevor Pearce, who injured his knee in the fall. For the eighth time the lifeboat closed in on the yacht, and it was the skipper's turn for rescue. When the last man was safe, the lifeboat turned towards home. There were seven men on board, so Frank slowly and carefully steered back through the stormy seas into harbour.

While Trevor Pearce was taken to hospital for treatment to his injured knee, the lifeboat was refuelled and made ready for service again. When the storm died down a fishing trawler brought the damaged yacht into Langstone Harbour.

Frank Dunster was awarded a bronze medal for his courage and skill. Trevor Pearce and Graham Wickham both received special letters of thanks. Their rescue work had only taken thirty-one minutes, and four lives had been saved!

Poem: *The wind*
I can get through a doorway without any key,
And strip the leaves from the great oak tree.
I can drive storm-clouds and shake tall towers,
Or steal through a garden and not wake the flowers.

Seas I can move and ships I can sink;
I can carry a house-top, or the scent of a pink.
When I am angry I can rave and riot;
And when I am spent, I lie quiet as quiet.
James Reeves

Hymns: *1* When I needed a neighbour were you there?
2 Glad that I live am I

Prayer: We remember how brave the lifeboat men are who go to sea to help sailors in danger. Dear God, help us to grow brave and strong. *Amen*

New Penlee lifeboat off St Michael's Mount, April 1983.
Photograph: Topham

46 Joey

Most children enjoy television and one of their favourite programmes is Blue Peter, which has given fun and interest to millions of children for over twenty years. When money was needed to help feed hungry families in other countries, or to buy a lifeboat for sea-rescue, or dogs for the blind, or a home for the homeless, children heard about it and were able to help through the programme. Collections of silver paper, used postage stamps, woollen socks — whatever was needed — arrived by the ton at the Blue Peter studios, and special bring-and-buy sales brought in millions of pounds.

The Blue Peter team were once told of the opening of four bungalows in the grounds of St Lawrence's Hospital. They had been built especially for handicapped people who had spent years in hospital, and all of them had been paid for by one of the patients. This patient was so badly handicapped he couldn't use his arms or legs, or even talk.

This story seemed so hard to believe that the Blue Peter team took their cameras and went to see for themselves.

They found that the patient, Joey Deacon, had been born a spastic. It was true that he couldn't use his arms or legs. When he was a baby his mother had looked after him very carefully. However she realised with sadness that he would never learn to talk like other children, although he could grunt and make sounds. Loving and caring for him as she did, she believed that even if Joey had a handicapped body, he could still have a clever mind. So she sat him in his chair outside their house, and later asked him how many cars had passed. Joey counted out the answer by blinking his eyes.

When his mother fell ill and died, Joey was six years old. His father couldn't both go to work and look after his two sons, so Joey went to live in a hospital. He was well looked after there, and his family came to visit when they could.

The hardest thing for Joey was not being able to talk, as because of this most people thought him simple-minded. Then a special doctor arrived, who showed Joey many different shapes. As the doctor called out, 'Triangle ... circle ... square ...' Joey pointed with his nose to the right shape. He gave the answers to addition and multiplication sums by blinking his eyes, and the doctor told Joey's father that his son was really very clever.

When Joey was twenty a wonderful thing happened. A man called Ernie came to live in the same ward, and for the first time ever someone understood the grunts and sounds that Joey made. The nurses didn't believe it at first, but Joey and Ernie soon proved it to be true, and became great friends. Two other men, Michael and Tom, came to their ward and the four men got on very well.

One day a nurse said to Joey, 'Why don't you write the story of your life?'

She meant it as a joke but Joey thought about it for a long, long time. Eventually he said to Ernie, 'I'm going to write my story.'

This was the start of another wonderful thing. Ernie found paper and pencil and Tom bought a typewriter. He couldn't read or write but he taught himself to type with one finger. Each day Joey made his grunts to Ernie, who watched his face and listened carefully. Then Ernie turned to Michael and repeated the words for him to write down. In the evening nurses read the work and put in capital letters, full stops, and corrected any spelling mistakes. Next day Joey held the script and grunted each letter to Ernie who called it out to Tom. As he typed, Tom repeated the letter aloud, adding their special code. So, as he typed the word 'work' he said, 'W for window, O for orange, R for Robert, K for kettle.'

It took a day to write three lines and a year and a half to finish the book. It was called *Joey*, and thousands of people in many countries read it and sent money to help the four friends. More wonderful things happened. Joey wanted two things especially in his life. One was to travel, the other was to live in a proper home. After writing this book Joey and his friends were able to have holidays in France, Switzerland and Holland. When a film was made from his story, the money paid for bungalows to be built in the hospital gardens. Joey's happiest dreams had come true.

Blue Peter told their viewers about Joey, and as usual the children helped. Bring-and-buy sales raised enough money to buy bungalows like Joey's, fifty electric cars like the one Ernie used, and many more aids for handicapped people. Perhaps the most valuable things they were able to buy were two incubators to look after very tiny new-born babies, to help them grow up strong and healthy, with no handicaps.

Poem: *Best of all*

I've got a lovely home,
With every single thing —
A mother and a father,
And a front-door bell to ring.
A dining room and kitchen,
Some bedrooms and a hall,
But the baby in the cradle
Is the nicest thing of all.

J. M. Westrup

Hymns: *1* Kumbayah
2 I'm very glad of God

Prayer: Dear God, we thank you for our blessings. Please help us to use our bodies and minds as well as we can today. *Amen*

47 An adventure in space

It must be a very exciting moment when an astronaut climbs into the spaceship that will take him far away from our earth and out into space. There is a count down: 10, 9, 8, 7, 6, 5, 4, 3, 2, 1! Then Blast-Off! and the great adventure begins.

A man in space
An astronaut had once set off
    Upon a long space flight;
The blast-off had been as it should
    And all was running right.

The world he knew was far behind,
    And there was nothing there
Except the meteorites which passed
    Like fireflies in the air.

Swiftly the ship hummed on through space;
    Sweetly the motors ran,
From time to time the astronaut
    His instruments would scan.

Yes, all was well; the craftsmen's work
    Was thorough and complete,
When all at once there came a jar —
    The engines missed a beat.

The man's heart missed a beat as well
    Was there some trouble then?
And here was he alone, alone,
    Far from the help of men.

Ah, he could see the trouble now,
    A little trembling rod,
The sign of something wrong below,
    He thought, Oh God, Oh God!

It was a very feeble prayer,
  Scarcely a prayer at all,
And yet he knew that something came
  In answer to his call.

He felt his heart grow full of peace
  He felt his fear had gone;
And then he saw a simple thing,
  That needed to be done.

On flew the spacecraft to its goal,
  The motors running free,
The spaceman thought, 'God's not out there;
  He's in my ship — with me!'

D. M. Prescott

Bible story: The Creation *Genesis* 1

Hymns: *1* God who made the earth
2 Praise him, praise him

Prayer: We thank you God for the wonderful world we live in.
Please help us to remember that you are always with us.   *Amen*

Useful reading: *Space age* by Reginald Turnill (F. Warne).

---

48   A picnic to remember

'How would you like to go on a picnic tomorrow, Ann? After all this
rain it would be lovely to get out. We could go to Camber Sands and
let the children enjoy themselves on the beach.'

Ann Palmer thought her neighbour's idea was great. 'I must talk
to the family first,' she said, 'but I'm sure they would love to come.'

So the Palmers and their two children Margaret and John agreed
to go with the Smith family for a day at the seaside.

The next day, Sunday, started in a damp misty way, not unusual
for the end of May, but everyone hoped that the sun would shine
for them later. The excited children helped to pack both cars with
picnic bags. Ann remembered a groundsheet for sitting on and the
boys brought cricket gear. Margaret insisted on taking the big
coloured beach ball she had been given for Christmas months ago.

Once on the beach the Smith boys ran off with John to organise a cricket game, while the grown-ups carried the picnic bags to a sheltered hollow in the sand dunes. Then everyone took turns to bat, bowl and field at cricket, shouting and laughing and getting very hungry! What a picnic they had — there were lots of different sandwiches, crisps, and some apples. The grown-ups had mugs of steaming hot tea and the children drank cans of coke.

Everyone enjoyed it so much that they didn't notice the noise at first.

'Someone's making a row,' complained Margaret.

A voice was yelling, 'Help! Help!' and someone screamed.

'Oh, it's only some lads playing around,' her mother replied.

Again they heard the cry, 'Help!'

John jumped up. 'I'm going to take a look,' he said, climbing to the top of the sandy hillock by pulling on the tall wild grasses which grew there.

'Quick,' he called. 'I'm sure it's serious!' They all ran across the sand dunes and followed him down to the beach. There they saw a deep hole dug in the sand. Nearby two boys were digging frantically into the wet sand, where the sides of another deep hole had fallen in. The picnickers were horrified to see a pair of ankles sticking out of the sand.

'Simon's in there!' one of the boys screamed as he dug.

The only thing to do was to claw at the sand and try to pull the boy out. Ann told Simon's two friends to go and call an ambulance. By desperate efforts the men managed to free the trapped boy. He looked deathly pale and Ann realised he had stopped breathing. Years ago, when she worked as an air stewardess, she had been taught how to give the 'kiss of life'. She wiped the sand from the boy's face and began to breathe into his mouth, until she felt his chest move and his breathing start again. The ambulance arrived, and Simon was wrapped in warm blankets and taken to hospital.

Later the families were to learn that the three boys had dug two holes. Simon had crawled into one to try and tunnel his way through to the other, so making a U shape. The wet sand had caved in and buried him up to his feet.

Ann Palmer hadn't heard the last of this adventure, however. To her surprise, a letter arrived asking her to go to the City Council Chambers where the Mayor of Chichester would present her with the Royal Humane Society's special award for saving a life. Someone else was also there to say 'thank you'. It was Simon, the boy rescued from the sand.

Song: *Dancing on the shore*

(*10 in a circle,* Ten little children dancing on the shore:
queen in centre) The queen waved a royal wand and out
went four.

(*4 step outside* Six little children dancing merrily;
circle) The queen waved a royal wand and out
went three.

(*3 step out and join* Three little children danced as children do;
hands with 4, The queen waved a royal wand and out
making an outside went two.
circle around
smaller one)

(*2 join larger* One little maiden, dancing just for fun;
circle) The queen waved a royal wand and out
went one.

M. M. Hutchinson

Hymns: *1* Glad that I live am I
2 Hands to work and feet to run

Prayer: Dear Father God, we remember the special days when we
have fun with our families and friends. When other people need our
help, may we be quick to give it. *Amen*

---

49 **The giant bear**

What is the name of our village, or our town, or our country? Have
you ever wondered why it was called by this name? It's always interesting to wonder about such things. Sometimes it is not very difficult
to find out, but sometimes you are given more than one answer!

When some Canadian children asked about the name of their
country — Canada — they found out that hundreds of years ago
Spanish explorers had sailed into Chaleur Bay. As the explorers
looked at the wild rocky cliffs they said to each other *aca nada*, which
means 'there is nothing here'. Other settlers came to those shores,
saw the huge forests, and thought no one could live happily in such
a wild country. But they were all wrong. For thousands of years many
groups of people had been living there in small villages. Each village
tribe found their food, clothes and shelter from the nearby wilderness.

The children also learned that people from many different countries had come to Canada and made it their home. When a man called Jacques Cartier explored their country in 1534, he wrote about people he met in the villages. The story goes that he called this new land Kanata (Kay-nah-tah), which is an Indian word meaning village.

The Canadian children were then taught some of the old stories that these settlers used to tell each other on dark winter nights; tales of ghosts and sailors, and of gold miners and wild animals. This is one of them — the story of a giant bear.

The giant bear

There once was a giant bear
who followed people for his prey.
He was so big he swallowed them whole.
Then they smothered to death inside him
if they hadn't already died of fright.
Either the bear attacked them on the run,
or if they crawled into a cave
where he could not squeeze his enormous bulk in,
he stabbed them with his whiskers like toothpicks,
drawing them out one by one,
and gulped them down.
No one knew what to do
until a wise man went out and let the bear swallow him
sliding right down his throat into the big, dark, hot,
  slimy stomach.
And once inside there, he took his knife
and simply cut him open,
killing him of course.
He carved a door in the bear's belly
and then he stepped out
and went home to get help with the butchering.
Everyone lived on bear meat for a long time.
That's the way it goes;
monster one minute, food the next.

Edward Field

After such a frightening tale, you might like this nonsense poem about a girl who met a bear. With her it was a very different story!

From *Adventures of Isabel*

Isabel met an enormous bear,
Isabel, Isabel didn't care;
The bear was hungry, the bear was ravenous,
The bear's big mouth was cruel and cavernous.
The bear said, Isabel, glad to meet you,
How do, Isabel, now I'll eat you!
Isabel, Isabel, didn't worry,
Isabel didn't scream or scurry.
She washed her hands and she straightened her hair up,
Then Isabel quietly ate the bear up.

Ogden Nash

Hymns: *1* God who made the earth
2 The ink is black, the page is white

Prayer: *From a Canadian school creed*

This is our school,
Let peace dwell here,
Let the room be full of contentment,
Let love abide here.
Love of one another,
Love of mankind,
Love of life itself,
And love of God.
Let us remember that as many hands build a house,
So many hearts make a school.   *Amen*

50   The astonishing tale of Caracole Frog

'I,' purred Velocity the leopard, tapping his furry chest with one sharp claw, 'am very strong, and I'm the fastest animal that ever lived!'

'Hah,' croaked Caracole Frog, jumping up and down excitedly. 'You leopards always say things like that, but I bet that I'm swifter than you.'

'What!' roared Velocity Leopard, almost falling backwards with surprise. 'Did I really hear that? Did I really hear you say that you are faster than me? Can't you see I'm much bigger than you, can't you use your eyes, you silly little frog!'

'So what if you are bigger than me, Velocity. You're a puffed-up lump of pride. I'll prove I'm faster than you,' said Caracole Frog argumentatively.

'Puffed-up lump of pride!' howled Velocity. 'I'll show you and then you'll see. We'll have a race and whoever gets to the finishing line first is the fastest,' he snarled in a confident way. No one had ever told the leopard that he could be beaten before. No one had ever dared.

Caracole Frog did a backward flip. 'I agree, whoever gets across the finishing line first is the fastest. Remember you said it. Whoever gets across the finishing line first is the fastest, no matter how it's done. Yes? Right?'

Velocity agreed, and the following day they met at the race track. Hoohoo the hyena was asked to stand at the starting line and to give the signal for the race to start. When Velocity arrived he began to do exercises. He flexed the muscles of his back legs ten times, then he did some stretching movements. Finally he jumped up and down twenty times. All the animals stood and watched. Velocity was smiling in a superior sort of way, but Caracole Frog stood quietly doing nothing. The frog seemed to be smiling secretly to herself.

'Come on, come on,' howled Hoohoo the hyena. Excited chatter rose amongst the animals, especially the monkeys, as Velocity and Caracole crouched, ready for the starting signal. Hoohoo gave a shriek of laughter — which was the signal to start — and they were off.

Velocity had years of training and practice and he ran with great skill. His breathing and stride were perfect, and his well-balanced muscles rippled as his long legs ate up the track with every leap. He was pleased with himself and enjoying the race.

As for Caracole Frog, she was on Velocity's back! She stood just behind his head, holding tight to his fur to keep herself from falling off. She was so small and light that Velocity didn't even notice.

Just before Velocity reached the finishing line, Caracole leaped off over the top of the leopard's head. She was still wearing her secretive smile.

'Yoo hoo,' croaked Caracole from across the finishing line. She grinned and waved to Velocity. 'So you've arrived at last. I've been waiting ages for you. I've proved I'm swifter than you, I think you will agree!'

'What-what-what ...' panted Velocity. His pale yellow eyes

almost leaped out of their sockets. He slumped to the ground, partly because he was tired from running the race and partly because of his astonishment. 'But, I know I'm faster ...'

'Ah, but we agreed, whoever crossed the finishing line first was the swiftest,' reminded Caracole Frog.

Corollary Rat was the judge and very, very solemnly he announced: 'Caracole Frog is the winner. She did cross the finishing line first.'

The animals had always said that Corollary Rat was a very fair judge so no one dared to argue. No wonder Caracole Frog still wore her secretive happy smile.

Poems: *A race*

A daisy and a buttercup
  Agreed to have a race,
A squirrel was to be the judge
  A mile off from the place.

The squirrel waited patiently
  Until the day was done —
Perhaps he is there waiting still,
  You see — they couldn't run.
Mrs Molesworth

A big turtle sat on the end of a log,
Watching a tadpole turn into a frog!

Sayings: More haste, less speed!
He laughs best who laughs last.

Bible reference: The one thing I do, however, is to forget what is behind me and do my best to reach what is ahead. So I run straight towards the goal in order to win the prize ... *Philippians* 3.13–14

Hymns: *1* I love God's tiny creatures
2 Give me joy in my heart

Prayer: Dear Father God, we thank you for the happy days we share together. Please help us in our work and play, always to do our best. *Amen*

---

51 The Queen's horses

Have you ever been to a wedding and listened to the bride and groom when they promise to love and look after each other for the rest of their lives? If you have, you will also have shared in the fun after-wards — the photographers at work, the wedding-breakfast and the celebrations. This happens at most weddings, but when the groom and his bride are the future King and Queen, then the celebrations are quite spectacular.

When Prince Charles and Lady Diana Spencer got married in 1981, not only their families and friends, but people from all over the world shared in the wedding celebrations. Hundreds of people were invited, and thousands more lined the London streets to see the parade and cheer when the royal carriages passed by. The crowds watched the Queen and her family and friends going to St Paul's Cathedral for the ceremony, then waited for their return to Buckingham Palace for the wedding celebrations. Millions of people all over the world could share their happiness by watching the wedding on television.

A seven-year-old girl called Debbie Spiller was one of the millions watching television that day. Like everyone else she saw the crowds in London, the carriages and the wedding guests, the bride in her billowing white gown with her new husband, the policemen on duty and the soldiers on guard — but Debbie especially enjoyed the sight of the beautiful black horses in the royal procession. At home Debbie took riding lessons on a brown pony called Scruffy. However, the sight of the soldiers in their dress uniforms mounted on their magnificent black horses gave her an idea.

'I should love to see those beautiful horses, Mummy,' she said. 'Do you think if I wrote to the Queen she would let me have a ride on one of them?'

'Well, I don't know about that,' replied her mother, 'but there's no harm in writing a letter and asking Her Majesty very politely.'

So that is just what Debbie did. She wrote to the Queen at Buckingham Palace in her best handwriting. Shortly afterwards a letter bearing the royal crest was delivered, addressed to Miss Debbie Spiller. A very excited Debbie opened the envelope carefully, anxious to know the reply. Her Majesty was pleased to receive Debbie's letter, but she regretted that it would not be possible to allow her to ride any of the horses, for if one person was allowed then many more would wish to do so. Debbie was invited to write to the Army Officer in command of the Household Cavalry in the Hyde Park Barracks. When she did this, the Captain replied, inviting her to come along on their next visitors' day. At least she would be able to see some of the fine horses that had taken part in the royal wedding day procession!

On the 21st April, 1982, more than six months since these letters, Debbie and her parents set off on the journey to London. They stayed the night in a hotel near Victoria Station. From here they could arrive at the barracks in plenty of time the following morning. That night the sound of trains in the busy station kept Debbie's mother awake, but Debbie was fast asleep. The excitement had worn her out, so not even the loudest train kept her from sleeping.

Debbie Spiller riding the Queen's horse, Octave.
Photograph: Southern Newspapers, PLC

After breakfast next morning the family left for the barracks. They were greeted by their soldier guide, looking very smart in black trousers and bright red jacket with shining gold buttons. He wore spotless white gloves and his black shoes shone with polish.

Together they watched a parade of the Queen's Lifeguards and listened to stirring music from the regimental band. Then everyone went to the stables to see the horses in their stalls. Each horse had its name engraved on a brass plaque above the stall. Debbie wanted to see the saddles, bridles, reins and stirrups in the tack-room, then in the forge they watched the blacksmith hammering a horse shoe on the anvil. To Debbie's surprise he invited her to strike the horse shoe while it was still hot.

The morning flew by until quarter past twelve, time for the visitors to leave the barracks, but Debbie's guide asked, 'Would you like to stay a little longer and have a ride on one of the horses?'

She gasped, 'Oh, yes please.'

The Guardsman lifted Debbie on to a black charger called Octave. She had been the favourite horse of Lord Louis Mountbatten, who used to call her Dolly. For a few minutes the little girl rode the great black charger, while cameras flashed and television cameras filmed her very special ride.

It had been an amazing visit to London. Back at school Debbie told everyone about her adventure, and showed them photographs of herself wearing a Guardsman's helmet and riding Octave. It was good to share with her friends a day she would always remember.

Hymns: *1* Go tell it to the mountains
2 When a knight won his spurs in the stories of old

Prayer: Father God, we remember all the joys we share. We thank you for the quiet days and the exciting days. Please help us to make today a good day.   *Amen*

52   The legend of the oriole

Patronella Johnston is an Ojibway. She was born on the Indian Cape Croker Reserve in North America. When she was a young girl, in the winter months she and several other children would stop on their way home from school at the home of a very old Indian lady, who lived to her one hundred and third year. They wanted to help her as she was so old and feeble, by bringing in kindling for her fire,

100

water to boil and frozen apples from the orchard. After the chores were finished they gathered around the hearth, where the old lady would bake apples for them and tell them an Indian story.

When Patronella grew up she went to Toronto and ran a boarding house for young Indians. To her surprise she discovered that they didn't know any of the stories she had been told. She wrote a book called *Tales of Nokomis*, so that other young Indians could learn the old legends and pass them on to their children. This is the legend of the oriole . . .

Nokomis was a very old woman. The cold made her ache all over, but now it was summer. The sky was blue, the sun bright, and little ripples on the lake sparkled like small drops of dew. The birds of the forest were singing all at once and the leaves of the trees were rustling in the wind.

Nokomis was going for a walk with her grandchildren, Bedabin and Tawa. Today they were going to the big hill about a mile away from camp, to look for wild flowers and berries. Both of them wanted to watch the birds, especially the orioles.

They had spent many hours lying flat on the ground beneath an elm tree, keeping as still as possible, to see these beautiful birds build their long nests and feed their young. The father bird was especially beautiful with his bright orange breast and deep black back. When the orioles build their nests they work very carefully, weaving fine twigs and grass in and out to make a strong home for their babies. Some nests would last for two or three years, they were so strong, but the birds only used them once. They made a nest in a different place the next year.

Tawa and Bedabin had tried very hard to look inside the nests. It was easy to climb the big elm, even up to the highest limb, but the orioles always built their nests away out on the very end of the branch and not even Tawa dared to climb out there.

Today they did not try to climb the elm, instead they lay quietly on the ground to watch the orioles feed their young. Nokomis sat down near them in the shade of an old tree and leaned against the trunk. She shut her eyes for a short nap.

The children lay quite still for a long time. When Nokomis woke up she rubbed her eyes. 'Do you know why the oriole is such a beautiful bird?' she asked with a smile.

'Weren't they always so beautiful?' Tawa asked.

'Oh no,' said Nokomis. 'At one time the oriole was a plain, grey little bird. His coat of grey was very dull but he had a beautiful voice and every morning he sang a song to greet the Sun as he came up over the edge of the forest.

'All the other birds ignored the plain little oriole. The poor bird felt quite lonely, but he kept on singing to the Sun each day. The Sun loved the oriole very much for the beautiful melody with which he greeted each morning. It made the Sun feel very joyous and he shone even more brightly than usual. One morning after the oriole had sung his song, the Sun said to him, "I wish to do something for you because you have been so friendly. I will grant you one wish. Think hard before you make it because there can be only one."

' "I wish to be beautiful," the oriole said at once. All his life he had wanted this and he knew right away what to say. The Sun said no more but went on his way further up the sky. Later in the day, when the Sun was almost directly overhead, the oriole flew over a pond. He looked into the still water and saw a beautiful orange and black bird. How surprised he was and how full of joy, he could hardly stop singing. "Now all the other birds will play with me and I won't be lonely any more," he sang joyfully.

'The next morning, because he was so grateful, he sang all the harder to greet the Sun, who was pleased at the small bird's joy and happy that the oriole had remembered to say thank you. He smiled warmly and said, "You are now beautiful on the outside, but your beautiful song and your beautiful nature give me even more pleasure. You will always remain lovely as long as you continue to sing your song to the world.

' "I will teach you how to build your nests in safe places out on the highest limbs, and no one will ever learn the secret of how you weave them there. In this way I will know that there will always be orioles to greet the sunrise." '

Hymns: *1* The golden cockerel
2 All things which live below the sky

Prayer: Thank you for the world so sweet,
Thank you for the food we eat,
Thank you for the birds that sing,
Thank you God for everything.
Amen

53   An ocean of stories — Kathasaritsagara

Kathasaritsagara means 'an ocean made up of rivers of stories'. It is one of the oldest collections of stories in the world and comes from India. (Some of the stories are to be found, wearing recognisable disguise, in the Arabian Nights.) There are stories of kings and demons, clever young men and beautiful young ladies, wicked plotters and happy simple folk, talking animals and magic mountains. Many of the stories have a hidden meaning. They are at their best when wickedness is discovered and punished and when goodness is rewarded, as in today's story.

Once upon a time, a long while ago and far away, there lived a mendicant. His home was a temple and he pretended to be a good and holy man. He also pretended that he was under a vow of silence. People came to visit him and pay their respects, and they brought gifts of clothes, food and money. Most of the gifts he kept for himself, but some he handed to his followers, who stayed around him calling themselves his disciples.

One day a rich merchant came to him with his wife and lovely daughter. The daughter was very beautiful indeed and the false mendicant wanted her to be his wife. Instead of talking to her father in the proper way he thought up a wicked plot.

He took the merchant aside and whispered, 'You know I have taken a vow of silence, but I must speak with you as I have your best interest at heart. It is about your daughter. She is very unlucky and if you keep her with you, your luck will desert you.'

'Oh dear, what shall I do?' the merchant asked, looking very anxious.

'It's simple,' replied the mendicant. 'What you must do is this. Put her in a casket and float it down the river tonight. Remember to put a lamp on the top of the casket.'

'Very well,' said the merchant.

Early that night a prince was crossing the river on his way back from a hunting expedition. Suddenly he saw a casket with a light on it floating downstream. With the help of his servants he hauled it on board his boat. When he opened the casket, he was amazed to discover a beautiful girl weeping inside. He comforted her gently and promised that no harm would come to her. The prince had a very fierce monkey that he had captured in the forest. The monkey was put into the casket, the lamp was re-lit, then it was left to float down the river.

On the river bank near the temple, the mendicant was eagerly waiting for the casket with the lamp. As soon as he saw it he ordered his followers to swim out and bring it to him. The casket was carried into his private room. Sending his followers away, he took a deep breath before opening the lid.

Before he knew what had happened a large bit of his nose was gone! Then it was his ear. Shrieking like a madman, he ran out and was never seen again. How could a beautiful girl change into such a savage monkey?

And of course, in time, the prince married the beautiful girl and they both lived happily ever after.

Poems:

Where
Monkeys in the forest,
Beggermen in rags,
Marrow in a knucklebone,
Gold in leather bags;

Dumplings in the oven
Fishes in a pool,
Flowers in a parlour,
Dunces in a school.

Feathers in a pillow,
Cattle in a shed,
Honey in a beehive,
And me in bed.
Walter de la Mare

Ferry me across the water
'Ferry me across the water,
    Do boatman do,'
'If you've a penny in your purse
    I'll ferry you.'

'I have a penny in my purse,
    And my eyes are blue;
So ferry me across the water,
    Do boatman, do.'

'Step into my ferry-boat,
    Be they black or blue,
And for the penny in your purse
    I'll ferry you.'
Christina Rossetti

Sayings: Some say: It's better to be born lucky than rich.

Jesus said: Fear not, I am with you always.

Hymns: *1* Can you count the stars?
2 Father hear the prayer we offer

Prayer: We thank thee, loving Father,
        For all thy tender care;
    For food and clothes and shelter,
        And all thy world so fair.
            Amen

Mendicant — member of religious order living entirely on alms.

54 Sajjan the robber

A long time ago in India there lived a robber called Sajjan. He was cruel, wicked and very greedy. Sajjan used his home as a resting place for travellers. He liked to make people think that he was a good and holy man. On one side of his home he built a mosque for Muslim travellers and on the other side he built a temple for Hindu visitors. He even dressed in the white robes that holy men wore and spread a prayer mat on his lawn.

Whenever Sajjan saw a rich-looking traveller he would smile in a friendly way and say, 'Do come and share my home tonight! I will prepare a feast for you to enjoy and give you a comfortable bed to lie on.'

When his unlucky guests were asleep Sajjan would creep into their rooms and kill them. Then he kept their money and jewels for himself.

One day Sajjan saw two travellers arriving. They looked so happy he thought they must be very rich!

'Good friends, you both look tired, do stay a night in my home,' he invited them warmly.

Guru Nanak was a teacher and a holy man and he was travelling with his old servant and friend, Mardana. Nanak had heard many whispers about the evil Sajjan, but he thanked him politely and added, 'It's true, we are rather tired and we would be happy to spend this night in your house.'

As always Sajjan made a feast of dainty dishes, then after they had finished eating, he remarked, 'See how late it is! Let us say goodnight now and go to bed.'

But Nanak didn't move. 'We never go to bed without first singing our hymns.'

Sajjan wasn't at all pleased to hear this, but he had to agree to sit down and listen as Nanak and Mardana began to sing:
> 'The white heron is found in holy places,
>> Yet it eats living things.
> The white heron is beautiful,
>> But its heart is evil.'

Sajjan sat motionless as the song went on. He thought to himself, 'I am like the white heron. I pretend to be kind to people but I steal from them. Like the white bird I too kill my prey, because I am so greedy.'

Suddenly he realised how wicked he had become, and he knew that Nanak had sung the hymn especially for him.

'Oh Nanak, I have been so wicked. Can you ever forgive me?' Sajjan fell on his knees and begged Nanak.

'Only God can forgive you,' replied Nanak. 'If you are truly sorry and take all you have stolen and give it to the poor, then God will forgive you.'

Sajjan did just that and he became a loyal follower of Guru Nanak. The very first Sikh temple in India was built by Sajjan, as his way of saying thank you to Nanak for changing his life.

Poem: *The Lord's name be praised*
Hey, all you children,
    Bless you the Lord!
All fathers and mothers,
    Sisters and brothers,
Praise him and magnify him for ever!

All you deeps of the ocean,
    Bless you the Lord!
All whales and porpoises,
    Turtles and tortoises,
Praise him and magnify him for ever!

All field mice and larder mice,
    Bless you the Lord!
All hedgehogs and moles,
    Rabbits and voles,
Praise him and magnify him for ever!

Let everything that hath life
    Praise the Lord!

Anon.

Hymns: *1* Glad that I live am I
2 The ink is black, the page is white

Prayer: Dear God, help us to grow strong; to speak the truth and to treat each other with kindness. *Amen*

Sajjan grew in personal faith, demonstrating the way of Sikhism — one of love of God and service to man.

55 Tejimola

Once there was a merchant who had a beautiful daughter called
Tejimola. Her mother died when she was a little girl and the
merchant married again. It made him happy to think that when he
needed to travel away from home on his trading trips, his new wife
would look after Tejimola for him.

Time passed and every day Tejimola grew more beautiful. She was
gentle and kind and all the village people spoke well of her. The
merchant loved his daughter dearly and always remembered to bring
her a special present when he returned from one of his trips to the
big cities.

Her stepmother became more and more jealous of Tejimola.

'Why should I do all the work in the house while Tejimola gets
such lovely presents?' she grumbled to herself.

So she started being unkind to her stepdaughter when the
merchant was not at home. 'You can do the work, girl. Wash the
clothes, then clean the house and after that you can go to market!'

When Tejimola was tired at the end of the day her stepmother
would say, 'Now go to bed — there's no supper left for you!'

The merchant was sad to learn that Tejimola was being treated like
this. He spoke to his wife about it, but there was no kind word from
her. Quietly he talked to Tejimola.

'This trip will be longer than usual, I am afraid. Before I go I have
something very special to give to you. It is the amulet that once
belonged to your dear mother. It is magic! Now put it on your arm
and if ever you are in trouble, it will tell you what to do.'

After the merchant had gone it wasn't long before the stepmother
began to illtreat Tejimola. They quarrelled and the girl was told she
must leave the house. Poor Tejimola! Where was she to go and what
could she do? Suddenly she remembered the magic amulet on her
arm.

'What shall I do now?' she asked it tearfully.

'I could take you to another land,' suggested the amulet.

'Oh no, I want to be here when my father returns,' she replied.

'I have another idea,' the amulet said. 'I shall turn you into a
melon plant until your father returns.'

Like magic, Tejimola disappeared and a beautiful melon plant
grew where she had been standing.

An old woman passing called to the stepmother, 'Please give an
old woman a melon!'

'If you can find a melon, you can have it,' was the reply, but when she went to pick one the plant called out:

'Don't touch this plant or danger will befall you!'

Surprised and frightened, the old woman went back to the house and shouted, 'You can keep your melon, I don't want any talking fruit!'

Then the stepmother guessed what had happened. The melon plant was growing just where she had last seen Tejimola weeping. Thinking that there must be some magic brewing, she pulled the plant out and threw it away.

By the next morning a fine grapefruit tree grew where the melon plant had been. Some boys passing by stopped to ask if they could have a grapefruit, but the same thing happened.

'Don't pick the fruit, or danger will befall you!' the tree cried.

They called out, 'Your tree is haunted!' and ran away as fast as they could. Again the stepmother guessed what had happened and cut down the tree.

The next day a beautiful waterlily was growing in that same spot. When the merchant returned home a few days later he put his hand out to pluck it.

'Father, it is I.'

The merchant was so surprised to hear his daughter's voice he hardly knew what to say.

'If you are Tejimola turn yourself into a bird and come into the house with me.' Straight away a small white bird flew on to his hand and together they went into the house.

As they entered, his wife came to greet him and she began to grumble about Tejimola.

'She is so rude and lazy and she never does any of the things I ask her to do!'

The father sighed, 'Oh dear, that doesn't sound like my Tejimola. Please ask her to come to me and I will speak to her.'

His wife replied, 'You can't do that, when I asked her to do some work she ran away.'

The merchant looked at the little bird. 'Is that what you did, Tejimola? Don't be afraid, take your human form and tell me if this is true.'

Then there was Tejimola standing before them both. As soon as the stepmother saw her, she fell at her husband's feet and begged to be forgiven for telling such lies and being so unkind.

Angrily the merchant told her she must go away for ever.

'Please, please,' the stepmother begged, 'I'm sorry, I really am.'

Tejimola was a kind-hearted girl. 'Father, let us forgive her,' she pleaded, and at last he agreed.

After that day the stepmother changed her ways and all three of them lived happily together.

Sayings: All's well that ends well! Forgive and forget.

Hymns: *1* The sun that shines across the sea
2 I have seen the golden sunshine

Prayer: Dear Father God, if we need to forgive anyone who has hurt us today, may we do so with goodwill, and help us to spread happiness in every way we can. *Amen*

---

56 The clever son

Parameswar was a moneylender, who had three wives. This used to be quite common in India, and many men had two or three wives.

Parameswar had three sons, Kittu, Pattu and Chota. The three boys were neither clever nor stupid. They were just rather ordinary boys. They were not particularly fond of reading or arithmetic and stopped going to school at an early age.

Parameswar began to worry because he was getting old, and he didn't want to leave his shop to all three sons. That would never do, for the boys would surely quarrel among themselves. He wanted to leave his shop to the one who was the cleverest.

His three wives talked to him, each wanting him to give the shop to her own son. They also quarrelled among themselves. The old man was very unhappy. How was he to find out which son was the cleverest, without fighting with his wives?

Then he thought of a way of deciding which son was the cleverest. He called the three boys before him and said, 'I'm giving each of you a rupee. Go out and buy something with the rupee which will entirely fill one of the rooms in our house.'

The first son, Kittu, bought a big cart-load of straw. In those days straw did not cost much and he got a lot for his rupee. Kittu loosened the strings of the bundles and filled his room with the loose straw.

Pattu, the second boy, bought a huge bale of waste cotton with his rupee. He opened the bale and the loose cotton filled his entire room.

The youngest son, Chota, changed the rupee for sixty-four copper pice. With one pice he bought a clay lamp; with another, a little oil; and with a third pice he bought some lampwick. The other sixty-one copper pice he knotted safely in a corner of his long shirt.

When Chota went to his room he poured the oil into the clay lamp, put in the wick, and lit the lamp from the kitchen fire. The little flame leapt up and lit the entire room brightly.

Parameswar and his three wives came to see how each son had filled up his room. When they opened the door to the first room they coughed and coughed because of the dust from the straw. Still coughing, they opened the door to the second room and then loose cotton flew into their mouths and eyes. Rubbing their eyes and still coughing they came to the third room. Young Chota stepped out to greet his father and to give him sixty-one copper pice, the change from his one rupee. His room was filled with light! And he had only spent three pice!

Parameswar and his wives all agreed that Chota was the cleverest of the boys and he deserved to run the shop. They had no doubt that he would be a very good and wise moneylender.

Poem: *The inheritance*
My mother she died, and she left me a reel,
A little silver thimble and a pretty spinning-wheel.
With a high down, derry O, derry O, derry O!
High down, derry O! dance o'er the broom.

I spun all day, and I sold my yarn,
And I put in my purse all the money I did earn;
And when at last I'd saved enough,
I bought me a gown of a pretty silver stuff.
A cap of gold, and a sash so gay!
'Oh what a pretty lady!' I heard the people say.

Had I been idle, then no doubt,
In rags, like a beggar, I'd wandered about;
With a high down, derry O, derry O, derry O!
High down, derry O! dance o'er the broom.
Anon.

Hymns: *1* Daisies are our silver, buttercups our gold
2 At half-past three we go home to tea

Prayer: We thank you Father God for all the gifts you have given us; eyes to see, ears to hear, minds to think, and especially we thank you for all the people who love and help us each day.   *Amen*

57 A prince is born

A long, long time ago in the high mountain lands of India, near the great city of Benares, a baby prince was born. His father was a king and a famous soldier. He was delighted to have a son and said, 'When he grows up, my son will be a great warrior and he will lead my army, driving our enemies away like sheep.'

The baby grew into a fine boy, but unlike other children he lived in a palace with servants to look after him. The palace had many beautiful gardens where the prince could play and around the gardens was a high wall. As he grew bigger his father taught the young prince how to use a spear and a sword. He wanted to make quite sure that his son would be a brave warrior when he grew up. But all the time the prince never left the palace grounds or went beyond the great wall that guarded them.

It was not until he was a young man that he persuaded his father to allow him to use the new palace chariot and go into the busy city of Benares, of which he had heard so much from travellers who visited the palace.

The chariot was made ready and the best of the palace drivers was chosen to stand beside the prince as he drove out through the great gates and on to the road that led to Benares. It was exciting to see so many people, and they waved when they recognised the chariot and the handsome young prince driving by.

Suddenly the chariot had to stop. An old man had stepped into the road and they had to wait for him to pass. How white his hair was! His back was so bent that every slow step seemed to be painful for him. The young prince had never seen such an old man. They hadn't gone much further when they were forced to stop the chariot again. This time four men were carrying a stretcher across the road. The chariot driver explained to the prince that they were carrying a man who had just died. As they waited for the men to pass, they could hear the sound of groaning, and the prince saw a man lying on the pavement. He looked in great pain and his face and body were hot and damp with fever.

Noticing how upset the prince was, the driver explained to him, 'We have seen a very old man and here you see a dead man and one who is very ill. If you look over there you will see a poor beggar. He sits holding his begging bowl, hoping that someone will give him some money for food. My prince, there is sadness in this world as well as happiness. It is the way of life!'

Never had the prince seen people in such trouble or met with such sadness. He suddenly felt he had seen enough and said, 'Let us go back to the palace now.'

After they returned to the peace and quiet of the palace gardens the prince had time to think. He could not forget the four men he had seen. For a long while he thought about them and felt sad for them. Then one day he made up his mind. He now knew that he could never be a warrior like his father. He must somehow find a way to help those people who were in trouble – whether they were old or sick, or whether they were poor, or just sad because someone that they loved was dead.

One night he said goodbye to his family and quietly left home. When he reached the limit of his father's land he changed from his princely clothes and put on a robe like his servants wore. He wandered on, across the countryside, until he came to a river. Close by he found a pipal tree and he sat beneath it. The prince made up his mind that he wouldn't move until somehow he could understand how he could help people to find happiness in life. He sat there all day and then all through the night. Gradually wise thoughts came to him, like a light shining into his mind. Now he knew what men must do to lead a good life.

He decided to travel around the country and teach people what he had learned. From that day people called him the Buddha, which means 'the one who knows'. The tree he had sat under was called the Bo tree, which means the 'tree of knowledge'. Today millions of people still follow his teachings.

Good advice: *An adaptation of the Buddha's Noble Eightfold Path*
You should — think the right thoughts,
               do things for a good reason,
               speak only the truth,
               behave as well as possible,
               care for all other living creatures,
               be as useful as possible,
               not act without thought,
               always try your hardest.

Hymns: *1* Glad that I live am I
2 For all the strength we have

Prayer: Dear God, in our work and in our play today please help us to do our very best. Thank you for the kindness of those who help us. May we do our best to be kind and helpful too. *Amen*

Buddha — Gautama Siddhartha – lived *c.* 560 BC. The Four Noble Truths and the Noble Eightfold Path are traditionally followed, as described in the first sermon of the Buddha.

(above)
Briton ordained as a
Buddhist monk, London.
Photograph: Topham

(right)
Bronze Buddha, Japan.
*Photograph: BBC Hulton
Picture Library*

58   Muhammad

A long time ago during the so-called 'Year of the Elephant', a baby boy was born in the city of Mecca in Arabia, a sandy desert land where it hardly ever rains and it is very hot.

The boy's name was Muhammad. Sadly, his mother and father both died before he was six, so for a while he lived with his grandfather and then he went to stay in his uncle's home. When he was old enough Muhammad learned to be a shepherd. He climbed the quiet hills with the other shepherds and together they looked after the sheep.

When he grew to be a young man Muhammad joined one of the camel caravans that travelled across the desert carrying goods from Africa or India to the markets of Arabia. He learned to ride camels, and he loved the way their long legs seemed to sail so smoothly across the miles of desert sand. He understood why people called these proud creatures the 'ships of the desert'.

When the caravans stopped at an oasis to let the people and animals have a rest and take water from the wells, they often met other travellers. It was good to talk together, and Muhammad liked listening to the Jews who told him stories about Noah, Abraham and Moses, and to the Christians with their tales of Jesus.

The men were friendly, and happy to share their food with strangers. They seemed so different from the rich men of Mecca. Although they danced and sang in praise of the sun, the moon and the stars and all their other gods, the rich only wanted to become richer and no one seemed to care what happened to poor people.

Muhammad enjoyed the life of a merchant, and in time he became leader of the caravans belonging to a rich lady called Khadija. She grew to love and trust him and eventually they were married.

After the long desert journeys with the camel caravans, when Muhammad came home to Mecca he liked to escape from the noise and dust of the city and climb up to the hills and the quiet caves that he had known as a shepherd boy. One day while he was peacefully sitting there, he seemed to see a huge figure in the sky. He thought he was seeing the Angel Gabriel. As the figure came closer it said, 'Read.' Muhammad was so frightened at first he didn't know what to do.

'Read,' the angel repeated – and then again said, 'Read.'

'But I can't read . . .' Muhammad replied.

'You will not read the books of men, but you will tell men the words that God speaks to you.'

When the figure had gone Muhammad didn't know what he should do. Had he been dreaming? Would people think he was mad? He decided to tell his wife and his cousin who was a Christian. They listened and believed him. They thought he had seen an angel and that God had chosen Muhammad to be his messenger.

After that day there were more messages, but only once more did Muhammad see the angel. He began to tell the people of Mecca about the messages from God. But the rich people of Mecca didn't want to believe that there was only one God, or to be told that they should treat poor people like their own brothers. They threw things at Muhammad in the street and even plotted to kill him. So Muhammad and his good friend Abu Bakr escaped from Mecca and made their way to the town of Medina about two hundred miles away.

The Jews and Christian people didn't want to change their ways, but many people did listen to Muhammad as he repeated the messages he had been given. He became a great leader and after eight years he was able to go back to Mecca. This time people did listen to him. One of the first things he did was to go to the great building called the Ka'ba and destroy all the old idols. He made it a holy place, fit to worship the God he called Allah. It is said that the only picture Muhammad did not destroy was the picture of Jesus and his mother Mary.

Hymns: *1* Morning has broken, like the first morning
2 The family of man

Prayer: *From a prayer of Muhammad*
Praise be to God who feeds us and gives us drink, who provides for us and shelters us.

After Muhammad died the messages given to him were written down in a book called the Qur'an. Today millions of people who call themselves Muslims read the messages; their faith is called Islam. The five laws of Islam are: faith in the one God called Allah; prayer, five times daily and facing to Mecca; charity; fasting at special times; and at least once in a lifetime a pilgrimage to Mecca. Muhammad said, 'Christians and Jews were the nearest in love to the believers in Islam.' Muslims believe that Adam, Noah, Abraham, Jacob, Moses and Jesus were also God's prophets, and that Muhammad is the last of the prophets.

59 A mountain to climb

It isn't every day that people climb a mountain carrying babies on their backs, but this is just what Sally and Ian did with their two young children on a beautiful sunny spring morning.

'Mummy, are we really going to climb the mountain today?' Shona asked as they ate an early breakfast in their tent. The family were camping on a site near Portmadoc in North Wales, not far from Snowdon.

'Yes, I hope so,' replied her mother, 'and there are lots of things to get ready, so we mustn't waste time.'

Already mother and father were dressed in tee shirts, breeches and the thick long socks that were comfortable for climbing. Ian packed the car with gear for the day while Sally dressed two-and-a-half year old Shona and her baby brother Stephen, ready for their adventure.

They had chosen to climb the Beddgelert Path on the south side of the mountain, rather than the Miners Path or the Pig Track which lay to the north. After a short drive they parked their old red Maxi by a farmyard.

Shona called in an excited voice, 'Look at all the sheep, Daddy!'

They watched as two black and white sheepdogs obeyed the shepherd's whistles and cleverly rounded up the flock, guiding the sheep through the farmyard and out to pasture.

Sally picked up baby Stephen and gently fitted him into the Papoose, a special sack which strapped on to her back.

'I've packed the waterproofs, jumpers and baby gear in the pockets of Stephen's sack,' she said.

Ian lifted his daughter into the other Papoose. He paused for a moment to check they had everything – compass and maps, food and drink, the survival bag and a supply of emergency chocolate. They were off!

At first their path led through fields. There were drystone walls to scramble over, cows to avoid, and stiles to cross.

'I'm feeling hot already,' gasped Sally. 'I know Stephen isn't nine months old yet, but he's getting heavy.'

Gradually the path became more difficult. They crossed streams and rocky gullies and all the time the track was becoming steeper. A steady climb brought them to the south ridge of Snowdon. It was almost half past twelve — time to stop for lunch.

What a relief to lift the children's sacks from their shoulders! The gentle breeze that welcomed them at the ridge was really refreshing. They all sat down on a rocky ledge and shared the picnic food. Never had cheese and tomato sandwiches tasted better. Stephen ate his baby-food hungrily — the mountain air had given even him a good appetite. Time for a nappy change, then the children were put back in their Papoose sacks and mother and father set off on the last part of their climb. The track was even steeper now and there were many other climbers out, some with children, a few with dogs, but no one else seemed to be carrying babies that day!

The path turned to the north and took them out on the ridge. Both the children slept in their sacks, as Sally and Ian worked their way steadily along the narrow ledge. The view was superb as they looked down on the beautiful Welsh valley, with the sunlight glinting on the lakes below. Brightly-coloured figures of other climbers could be clearly seen on various paths up the mountain side. There was just a last steep climb over some large loose rocks, and at last they reached the summit. It was early afternoon and the climb had taken them three hours.

The distant views were as beautiful as they expected, but Snowdon wasn't like mountains they had climbed in the past – not deserted, with a wild silent beauty. Here they found a small station! The mountain railway from Llanberis on the north side brings visitors to the summit terminus. Both children had woken up, and Shona was thrilled to see a train at the little station. Crowds of people spilled from the carriages. Judging from their variety of speech and dress, they must have come from all over the world.

The one thing the family had forgotten to bring was money. Usually there is no need for money on a mountain climb, so it was no use looking at ice creams for sale in the small café! Instead they left the summit and walked a short way back along their path until they came to a grassy plateau. It was peaceful there, and the children played in the sun for a while as Sally and Ian enjoyed the view and a quiet rest.

Then once again the children were put in the Papoose sacks and the family started their homeward journey, stopping half-way down the mountain when Stephen began to get tired. His mother him gave a cuddle and a share of the chocolate, then for the last hour of the downward climb they sang songs to keep him happy and played 'I spy sheep'.

At the car they found money to buy ice creams from the farm then drove back to camp, tired but happy. It had been a good day's climb for Sally and Ian, and a real adventure for two young Papoose travellers!

Hymns: *1* Go tell it to the mountains
2 For the beauty of the earth

Prayer: We thank you Father God, for beautiful mountains
and happy sunny days.
Please help us on our way today and keep us safely
as we work and play.   *Amen*

60 The school year is over

The end of the summer term is almost here, and the end of another
school year. It's time to put our books away, tidy the classrooms and
say goodbye. The holidays have come once more and for a while we
shall each go our own way.

Soon there will be time for different things. Time to go away with
our families and see new places; time to play with friends; time to
meet new faces. At last we can do some of the things we enjoy 'when
we have the time', like the little boy who loved to go fishing . . .

Boy and fish
The sun is bright and clear, fish.
Thank you, we can see it, boy.
The sand is soft and warm, fish.
We don't care a bit, boy.
My feet are making rings, fish.
We can make them, too, boy.
I'm looking hard at you, fish.
We're looking hard at you, boy.
I have a little net, fish.
So that's your little plan, boy.
I'm going to catch you now, fish.
Well, catch us if you can, boy.
I have a bucket here, fish.
Then fill it to the top, boy.
There's room for all of you, fish.
We really cannot stop, boy.
Tomorrow I'll be back, fish.
Tomorrow we'll be here, boy.
I'll have another try, fish.
The sun is bright and clear, boy.
Leonard Clark

In the holidays there will be time to try again, whether it's with fishing, swimming, cycling or working at things we choose to do. Like the girl in this poem, we shall have time to try, try, try again . . .

I tried

I tried to do some knitting,
I tried and tried and tried.
But all the holes and knots and things,
I just couldn't hide.

I tried to do some painting,
An Indian, colours bright.
Then my paint brush slipped, it smudged my work
So that it didn't turn out right.

I tried to do some sewing,
An apron or perhaps a scarf.
The scissors slipped,
And then I found, I'd cut my work in half.

So now I've turned to cooking,
I hope I will succeed.
Eggs, sugar, milk and flour,
These are the things I'll need.

Well, I tried.

Diane Lewis (age 11)

Hymns: *1* The ink is black, the page is white
2 Glad that I live am I
3 Day by day

Prayer: God bless the people of our school,
        Bless the helpers, the teachers and all the children;
    God bless our lessons and our learning,
        Bless our play and all our friends;
    God bless those who leave our school today,
        Bless them in all their future ways;
    God bless our holidays, keep us safely,
        Bless us till we meet again.
    For all our blessings, heavenly Father
    We praise and thank you, today and always.

Amen

The class assembly

'It's our turn to take assembly next week!' The following twenty assemblies are devoted to the many teachers who share this challenge with their classes.

A thematic approach is assumed and suggestions for development of each theme are provided, plus a selection of possible complementary material — stories, songs, poems, hymns, prayers, background music and visual aids. Sources are given either in situ or acknowledged on pages 214–15.

The following are some practical guidelines for those teachers who are meeting the responsibility of a class assembly for the first time.

Advance preparation is the secret of success. The starting point should be an awareness of the needs and characteristics of a class, the ethos and tradition of the school, and of course the teacher's personal approach to life. These factors will influence the various decisions to be made, such as:

1 Format
The school tradition is the obvious consideration, but a typical and suitable format is:
greeting/welcome/introduction of theme
hymn/song
presentation of children's work
prayer/meditation — based on thoughts and responses evolved from work on the theme
hymn/song.

2 Theme
There is a choice of using the current centre of interest of the class or of selecting a special theme for the occasion. The following pages contain suggestions for twenty suitable themes, with a wealth of material that can be adapted as required, using the index on page 211 as a guide to planning.

3 Development of theme
Background classroom work will contribute greatly towards a successful class assembly. Children's interest will be stimulated, so that their learning will be enjoyable and satisfying for the school, as well as for the class concerned. Their needs will be met, the central thought developed, and a response encouraged from the rest of the school.

Perhaps the most natural and popular form of expression will be through the medium of art. Children's work may form a colourful backcloth, or be used more specifically to illustrate a point during the assembly. Decisions concerning size, technique and presentation will vary enormously, for example the work may be the product of one child, a group, or that of the whole class. Suggestions are also made on suitable prints to illustrate each theme, from old masters to modern posters, or similar magazine pictures can of course be chosen.

A class assembly is an opportunity for children to display their craft work, from group projects (e.g. giant totem-pole) to individual clay figures. Other items for display could be clock faces, mobiles, charts, graphs, histograms, costumes, science experiments, etc. — the possibilities are endless.

The children could relate a story or poem through drama, mime, dance or movement; or sing, recite and play musical instruments — either solo, as a group, or as a class — using their own creative work or material selected from the suggestions given. They may wish to explain some aspect of their study of the theme, presenting the thoughts that have developed and demonstrating their response.

4 Hymns and songs

The first lines of suitable hymns and songs are given, but the class will undoubtedly have plenty of ideas of their own, as all schools enjoy a good repertoire. There is usually competition for the honour of choosing the music and announcing the hymns.

5 Prayer and meditation

This is perhaps the most important outcome of the whole endeavour. A meaningful prayer should be based on the children's thoughts developed while working on the theme, expressed fairly briefly in simple language. Suggestions are given at the end of each class assembly, but teachers or children may prefer to write their own, or to use a prayer familiar to the school.

6 Background music

The choice is of course personal, but suggestions have again been made relevant to the theme.

7 Practice run-through

The final part of preparation should be a practice session. To avoid identifying the assembly as a performance, one rejects the word 'rehearsal', yet a run-through is an extremely helpful part of preparation.

8 Setting the scene

The environment needs to be ready, with pictures, models, equipment, flowers, etc., all organised. Most children find security in knowing their 'places' and need practice and help when speaking to the school. A script may give them confidence, even though the majority of children learn their words without difficulty. If the script has suffered from a week's handling, making a new copy for 'the day' is time well spent.

An assembly takes shape under a teacher's guidance, but experience will prove that as children's involvement increases, they will happily accept their share of responsibility. A class assembly will then reflect all the talents, enthusiasm and vitality of both teacher and children, making it an event to be shared with pleasure by the rest of the school.

61 Day and night

Ideas on theme:
Pattern of day and night, characteristics of both. Language involved
— sunrise, dawn, etc. Greetings — good morning, good night.

Explanation of the earth's movement in relation to the sun, moon,
stars — phases of the moon, comets, tides. Land of the Midnight
Sun. Signs of the zodiac.

Measurement of day and night — time in hours, days, months,
calendars, clock faces to record special events, histogram of children's birthday months.

Lighting — naturally by sun, moon, stars . . . artificially from
candlelight to electricity. Special lighting — lighthouses, street
lighting, lamplighters. The need for light. The gift of eyesight. The
Olympic torch. Safety — in the dark, on the roads, traffic lights.

Effect of day and night in our lives — daily pattern of life for ourselves and for the less fortunate, e.g. the homeless. Night-workers —
hospital staff, doctors on night call, transport workers, emergency
services, space travellers.

Theme reflected in religion: Jesus said, 'I am the light of the
world.' Advent — start of Christian festival of light. Diwali — Hindu
and Sikh New Festival of Light. Hanukkah — Jewish festival.

Stories: The sun and wind boast about which has greater power,
and decide to test their skill on a man climbing a hill. When the wind
blows his hardest the traveller snuggles into his coat, but when the
sun shines he succeeds in making the man take off his coat. 'Sun and
wind', Wide Range series, *Blue 1*.

Daedalus, a skilled Athenian craftsman, built the Labyrinth for
King Minos of Crete. When he later incurred the King's displeasure
and had to flee, Daedalus made wings for himself and his son Icarus
and they flew from the island. Daedalus escaped, but Icarus flew too
near the sun, which melted the wax that fastened his wings, so he
fell into the sea and drowned. *Greek myth*

Paul's conversion *Acts* 22.6–16, Joseph's dream *Genesis* 37.10.

Poems:

The falling star

I saw a star slide down the sky,
Blinding the north as it went by,
Too burning and too quick to hold;
Too lovely to be bought or sold,
Good only to make wishes on
And then forever to be gone.

                    Sara Teasdale

The man in the moon

The man in the moon, as he sails in the sky,
    Is a very remarkable skipper;
But he made a mistake when he tried to take
    A drink of milk from the Dipper.
He dipped it into the Milky Way,
    And slowly and carefully filled it;
The Big Bear growled, and the Little Bear howled,
    And scared him so that he spilled it.

                    Anon.

Shiny

Shiny are the chestnut leaves before they unfold
The inside of a buttercup is like polished gold
A pool in the sunshine is bright too
And a fine silver shilling when it's new.
But the round full moon so clear and white
How brightly she shines on a winter's night!
Slowly she rises higher and higher
With a cold clear light like ice on fire.

                    James Reeves

A spike of green

When I went out
The sun was hot.
It shone upon
My flower pot.

And there I saw
A spike of green
That one no one else
Had ever seen!

On other days
The things I see
Are mostly old
Except for me.

But this green spike
So new and small
Had never yet
Been seen at all.

                    B. Baker

123

The moon

The moon has a face like the clock in the hall:
She shines on thieves on the garden wall,
On streets and fields and harbour quays,
And birdies asleep in the forks of the trees.

The squalling cat and the squeaking mouse,
The howling dog by the door of the house,
The bat that lies in bed at noon,
All love to be out by the light of the moon.

But all of the things that belong to the day
Cuddle to sleep to be out of her way;
And flowers and children close their eyes
Till up in the morning the sun shall arise.

R. L. Stevenson

Shining things

I love all shining things — the lovely moon,
The silver stars at night, gold sun at noon,
A glowing rainbow in a stormy sky,
Or bright clouds hurrying when wind goes by.
The beauty of all shining things is yours and mine.
It was a lovely thought of God to make things shine.

E. Gould

Sayings:

Early to bed and early to rise
Makes a man healthy, wealthy
and wise.

Evening red and morning gray
  It is the sign of a bonny day.
Evening gray and morning red
    The lamb and ewe go wet to bed.
Evening red and morning gray
  Set the traveller on his way.
But evening gray and morning red
  Bring the rain upon his head.

Rainbow at night
  is the sailor's delight.
Rainbow at morning
  sailors take warning.

A sunshiny shower
Won't last half an hour.

Three things cannot long be hidden,
The sun, the moon, and the truth.   *Buddha*

Hymns: *1* Thank you for every good new morning
2 I love the sun
3 Morning has broken, like the first morning
4 When lamps are lighted in the town
5 The sun that shines across the sea

Music: Dvorak, *Symphony no. 9 (New world)*
Holst, *Planet suite*
Grieg, *Peer Gynt suite (Dawn)*
Strauss, *Thunder and lightning polka*

Pictures: Holman Hunt, *The light of the world*
Per Dahl, *Twilight hour*
Captain Scott, *Schooner*

A final thought — How the pattern of day and night is fundamental to our lives.

Response: Awe, praise, thanksgiving.

Prayer: Dear God, we thank you for the wonderful world we live in; for the warmth of the sun by day and the light of the moon at night. Today help us to light someone's life with our kindness.

Amen

62   A baby in the family

Ideas on theme:
Baby — a very young child, unable to walk or talk, youngest member of the family, babyhood, babysit, baby grand (piano).

A new baby — preparation, birth, boy or girl, christening. Choosing a name — Christian name, surnames, favourite/popular names, histogram of class names.

Relationships — mother, father, grandparents, brothers, sisters, family. Only child, twins, triplets, etc.

Special needs — loving care, baby foods, high-chair, cradle, cot, pram. Baby clothes — layette, baby-grow, significant colours (blue for a boy, pink for a girl).

Toys — soft toys, rag-books, picture stories, games from traditional toys to activity centres, baby dolls. Baby music — lullabies, counting songs. Baby games — pat-a-cake, this little piggy.

Learning to move — sit, stand, crawl, walk. Learning to talk — baby sounds, first words, learning to listen.

Animal/bird babies — special names (puppy, cygnet), homes (kennel, nest).

Plant life — seed, seedling, plant, flower, fruit.

Stories: Long ago in Holland, there lived a rich man who wanted to build a church in his town. He could not decide whether to put a tower or a spire on the top. When the church was partly built, he decided to go on a pilgrimage to the Holy Land. By that time, his wife was expecting a baby.

'If the baby is a boy,' said the man, 'finish the church with a spire, but if it is a girl, build a tower instead. Then I shall see it on my return journey when I am still far out at sea.'

The months passed, and twin boys were born, so their mother had two spires built side by side on the church. The church with its twin spires can still be seen. ('Boy or girl', Wide Range series, *Red 4.*)

Also from Wide Range series: 'Strange little duck' *Blue 2*, 'Little elephant who couldn't find his tusks' *Green 1*, 'Baby King' *Green 2*, 'Branch baby' *Red 2*, 'Little boy lost' *Red 6*, 'Teddy bears' *Interest 1*, 'Peter the pelican' *New Interest 3*, 'Three miracles' *More Interest 1*, 'A Greek boy' *History 1*.

Babes in the wood, Rumpelstiltskin, Goldilocks and the three bears, Baby Jesus, Moses, Solomon judges between two mothers both claiming baby boy (*1 Kings* 3.16–28).

Lullabies: Golden slumbers kiss your eyes,
     Smiles awake you when you rise,
 Sleep pretty baby, do not cry,
     And I will sing a lullaby;
       Lullaby, lullaby,
 And I will sing a lullaby!

Lullaby for an African baby
Someone would like to have you for her child
     but you are mine.
Someone would like to rear you on a costly mat
     but you are mine.
Someone would like to place you on a camel blanket
     but you are mine.
I have you to rear on a torn old mat.
Someone would like to have you as her child
     but you are mine.

Lullaby for a caterpillar

Sleep little caterpillar,
Soft, downy caterpillar,
Roll yourself up in a tender leaf.

Spin, spin your silken cover,
Spin little caterpillar,
Spin! Spin! Spin!

First, just close your eyes –
Wait for a big surprise
You will awaken a butterfly.

Sleep little caterpillar,
Soft, downy caterpillar,
Sleep! Sleep! Sleep!

Poems and rhymes:

What does the bee do?

What does the bee do?
  Bring home honey.
What does father do?
  Bring home the money.
And what does mother do?
  Lay out the money.
And what does baby do?
  Eat up the honey.
                    Christina Rossetti

What are little boys made of?
What are little boys made of?
  Snips and snails
  And puppy-dogs' tails,
That's what little boys are made of.

What are little girls made of?
What are little girls made of?
  Sugar and spice
  And all that's nice,
That's what little girls are made of.

Also: *Monday's child is fair of face*
Little Bo Peep
Diddle Diddle dumpling, my son John
I had a little nut tree

Little

I am the sister of him
  And he is my brother.
He is too little for us
  To talk to each other.
So every morning I show him
  My doll and my book;
But every morning he still is
  Too little to look.
                    Dorothy Aldis

Little girl, little girl,
  Where have you been?
'Gathering roses
  To give to the Queen.'
'Little girl, little girl,
  What gave she you?'
'She gave me a diamond
  As big as my shoe.'
                    Anon.

Sayings: Where did you come from, baby dear?
             Out of the everywhere into here!
                    G. Macdonald

Hymns: *1* I love God's tiny creatures
2 Praise him, praise him
3 All things bright and beautiful
4 Away in a manger

Music: Roger Quilter, *Children's overture*
Little Jesus sweetly sleep
Unto us a babe is born
Sweetest little fella, mighty like a rose

Pictures: Picasso, *Child and dove*
Leonardo da Vinci, *Virgin and child* or Raphael, *Madonna and child*
United Nations poster (Athena)

A final thought — The gift of life, the most precious gift of all.

Response: Praise and thanksgiving.

Prayer: From *Prayers in poetry*
Holy God, who madest me
And all things else to worship thee;
Keep me fit in mind and heart,
Body and soul to take my part.
Fit to stand, fit to run,
Fit for sorrow, fit for fun,
Fit to work and fit to play,
Fit to face life day by day;
Holy God, who madest me,
Make me fit to worship thee.   *Amen*

---

63   Mothers and fathers

Ideas on theme:
Mothers and fathers, parents, single-parent families, orphans.

Special days – to remember their love and care, an opportunity of saying thank you, to give a small gift. Mothering Sunday (fourth Sunday in Lent) when Christians revisit mother church and return to family home, bringing gifts for mother (traditionally a bunch of violets and simnel cake). Fathers' Day (usually third Sunday in June).

Various roles that parents play in their care of children — cook (preparation of food), nurse (sickness and first aid), home-maker (provider, laundry, cleaning), mechanic (mending toys), police (discipline), teacher (of many skills), sewer and knitter (making clothes), banker (pocket money), chauffeur, librarian, friend.

The traditional roles of mother and father – modern roles changing, both parents working, unemployment, ways in which children can help.

The Royal Family, kings and queens.

Special names in animal/bird kingdom – stallion, mare, foal/cock, hen, chicken.

Stories: The ugly duckling, Goldilocks and the three bears, Mother Teresa of Calcutta (see page 145), Moses in the bulrushes, Mary and Jesus.

From Wide Range series: 'Strange little duck' *Blue 2*, 'The miller, his son and the donkey' *Green 2*, 'Little barge girl' *Green 3*, 'A swan for the winter' *Red 1*, 'The golden broom' *Red 2*, 'A tree for the roof' *Red 3*, 'Clap hands Joanne', 'The school on wheels' *Red 5*.

Poems and rhymes:

Our mother

Hundreds of stars in the pretty sky,
Hundreds of shells on the shore together,
Hundreds of birds that go singing by,
Hundreds of birds in the sunny weather.

Hundreds of dewdrops to greet the dawn,
Hundreds of bees in the purple clover,
Hundreds of butterflies on the lawn,
But only one mother the wide world over.

Anon.

Mother's helper

I am Mother's helper,
I help her every day,
By dusting all the furniture
And putting things away.

I keep my cupboard tidy,
I help to make my bed;
I run on errands to the store
For butter and for bread.

And sometimes after eating,
I wipe the dishes too,
Why, Mother says without me
She can't think what she'd do.

W. C. Neilson

My mother

Who ran to help me when I fell,
And would some pretty story tell,
Or kiss the place to make it well?
My mother.

A. Taylor

The Christ Child

The Christ Child stood at Mary's knee,
His hair was like a crown,
And all the flowers looked up at him,
And all the stars looked down.

G. K. Chesterton

My father's hands

My father's hands are beautiful, they can fix this moth's
  wing and make machines
They can mend the fuse when the world goes dark
Can make the light swim and walls jump in around me again
I can see my mother's face again.

Never let blades or anything sharp and hurtful near them
Don't let bees or nettles sting them
Don't let fire or burning oil try them.

My father's hands are beautiful, take good care of them.

Jeni Couzyn

Lullaby

Hush, little baby, don't say a word,
Papa's going to buy you a mocking bird.

If the mocking bird won't sing,
Papa's going to buy you a diamond ring.

If the diamond ring turns to brass,
Papa's going to buy you a looking glass.

If the looking glass gets broke,
Papa's going to buy you a billy-goat.

If that billy-goat runs away,
Papa's going to buy you another today.

Anon.

Request number

Tell me a story, Father, please do;
  I've kissed Mama and I've said my prayers,
And I bade good night to the soft pussy-cat
  And the little grey mouse that lives under the stairs.

Tell me a story, Father, please do,
  Of power-crazed vampires of monstrous size,
Of hordes of malevolent man-eating crabs
  And pea-green zombies with X-ray eyes.

G. N. Sprod

Also: *There was an old woman who lived in a shoe*
Old Mother Hubbard   *Jack Sprat could eat no fat*
As I was going to St Ives   *Peter, Peter, pumpkin eater*

Sayings: God could not be everywhere and therefore he made mothers. *Jewish proverb*
Respect your father and mother, so that you may live a long time in the land that I am giving you. (The Fifth Commandment God gave to Moses *Exodus* 20.12)

Prayer: Our Father, who art in heaven . . .

Hymns: *1* Unto us a boy is born
2 At half-past three we go home to tea
3 God has given us a book full of stories
4 Can you count the stars?

Music: *The virgin Mary had a baby boy*
Ravel, *Mother Goose suite*

Pictures: K. Jakobsen, *Adam and Eve*
Leonardo da Vinci, *Virgin and child*
Family portrait, Family at the seaside (cats) (Athena)

A final thought — One of the greatest blessings any person can have in life is loving, caring parents.

Response: How can we show our appreciation and prove our love?

Prayer: Thank you for our mothers and fathers and for all they do for us. Please help us today to find a way to show our love for them.   *Amen*

64   Sisters and brothers

Ideas on theme:
Sister — daughter of same parent, woman who is a very close friend, fellow member of class, human race, member of religious community.

Brother — son of same parent, man who is a very close friend, fellow citizen, countryman, associate or equal.

Brethren — fellow members of religious society, union, regiment.

Position in family — eldest, youngest, middle. Other relationships — step-brother/sister, brother/sister-in-law, children of brothers and sisters, family tree, the school 'family' tree.

New baby in family — twins, triplets. Family characteristics — bodily, facially, colouring, temperament, names, class comparison of family sizes.

Shared pleasures of brothers and sisters — parents, home, toys, events, friendship, work, play. Disadvantages? Emotions between brothers and sisters — love, anger, jealousy, forgiveness.

Brotherhood of man — irrespective of colour, race or creed.

Stories: Four hundred years ago, Albert and Franz Dürer were brothers in a very large family. Although the two boys wanted to be artists, there was not enough money for them both to study with the great masters. They had the idea that one of them should study painting while the other earned money, then they would change over. That way they could both become artists. Albert was the younger and the better painter, so he had the first chance to learn. While Franz worked, Albert studied. When it was time for the two to change places, Franz' hands were so scarred with hard work that he could no longer paint. Albert thought of the best way to repay Franz — he painted a picture of his hands. *The praying hands*, by Dürer, is now a world-famous painting.

Martha and Mary *Luke* 10.38–42, Friends of Jesus (Simon and Andrew, James and John), Moses and his sister, Father Damien and the lepers, St Francis stories, Florence Nightingale, Cinderella.

From Wide Range series: 'Lok and Shan' *Blue 3*, *Red 3*, 'The boys who made aeroplanes' *Blue 4*, 'The run for Oklahoma' *Blue 6*, 'The school on wheels' *Red 5*, 'The great St Bernard Pass', 'The man who played Mother Bear' *Interest 3*, 'Day to remember' *More Interest 2*, 'The winter of '54' (Florence Nightingale) *History 4*.

Poems and rhymes:
Grey brothers
The grey goat grazed on the hill,
 The grey hare grazed by his side,
And never a word they said
 From morning till eventide.
And never a word they said,
 Though each understood the other,
For the wind that played on the hill
 Whispered, 'My dear grey brother.'

The grey goat went home at dusk,
 Down to the cottage door;
The grey hare scuttled away
 To his burrow across the moor.
And never a word they said,
 Though each understood the other,
For the wind that slept on the hill
 Murmured, 'Good night, grey brother.'
      A. M. Montgomery

Also: *Little* (Dorothy Aldis) See page 127.
Rabbit and Lark (James Reeves) See page 33.

Brothers and sisters
I quarrelled with my brother,
I don't know what about,
One thing led to another
And somehow we fell out.
The start of it was slight,
The end of it was strong,
He said he was right,
I knew he was wrong.

We hated one another.
The afternoon turned black.
Then suddenly my brother
Thumped me on the back,
And said, 'Oh COME along!
We can't go on all night –
I was in the wrong.'
So he was in the right.

Eleanor Farjeon

Little Betty Blue
Little Betty Blue
Has a button on her shoe;
But she's too fat to button it,
So what can Betty do?

She can ask her brother Paul
Who is rather thin and small;
Then he will come and button it
Without a fuss at all.

A. G. Herbertson

Three silly sisters
I only have two sisters,
I've loved them all my life.
They may think I don't mean it,
But I'd guard them with my life.
We fought a lot as children,
We even do today;
I love my silly sisters
No matter what they say!

Three riddles
I have a little sister. They call her Peep-peep;
She wades the waters deep, deep, deep;
She climbs the mountains high, high, high;
Poor little creature, she has but one eye.

Answer: A star

Two brothers we are,
Great burdens we bear,
On which we are bitterly pressed;
The truth is to say,
We are full all the day,
And empty when we go to rest.

Answer: A pair of shoes

They chose me from my brother: 'That's the
Nicest one,' they said,
And they carved me out a face and put a
Candle in my head;
And they set me on the doorstep. Oh, the
Night was dark and wild;
But when they lit the candle, then I
Smiled!

Answer: A Hallowe'en pumpkin
(*Dorothy Aldis*)

Bible reference: Jesus said, 'Who is my mother, and who are my
brothers?' With a gesture of his hand towards his disciples he went
on, 'There are my mother and brothers: for whoever does the will
of my heavenly Father is brother and sister and mother to
me.' *Matthew 12.48–50*

Hymns: *1* Jesus, good above all other
2 At half-past three we go home to tea
3 Kumbayah
4 The family of man
5 The ink is black, the page is white

Music: Dvorak, *Symphony no. 9 (New world)*
When I needed a neighbour were you there?
Boys and girls come out to play
Sisters
Two little girls in blue

Pictures: Dürer, *The praying hands*
Curious kittens, Pigs, United Nations (Athena)

A final thought — Brotherly (sisterly) love increases family peace.

Response: The same brotherly (sisterly) love will increase peace
for the greater family of man.

Prayer: Hey, all you children,
Bless you the Lord!
All fathers and mothers
Sisters and brothers,
Praise him and thank him for everything!

Amen
Anon. (*adapted*)

65 Toys, toys, toys

Ideas on theme:
Definition of toy – something to play with, especially for children, meant for amusement rather than serious use. Educational toys.

Toys for every age and interest. For babies — soft toys, teddy bears, pull-along toys, noisy toys, bath toys. For girls or boys, or both? — dolls, prams, houses, forts, toy soldiers, animals, bikes, cars, planes, boats, toys associated with TV characters, computer and video games. Histogram of favourite toys.

Construction toys — bricks, Lego, Meccano, model cars, ships, planes.

Outdoor toys — swings, climbing towers, sand and water, buckets and spades, bikes, skates.

Creative play — painting, drawing, clay modelling. Make believe — dressing up, cowboys, Indians, nurses, astronauts, etc. Musical games — drums, xylophones, musical boxes, kazoos. Sport — bats, balls, fishing tackle, boxing gloves, skipping ropes.

Materials used in making toys. Toy power — hand-propelled, clockwork, battery, mains. Care of toys, the toy hospital.

The history of toys. Toys at home, in school, in the park. For use alone, with a friend, the family, the 'gang'. Play without toys, or with pretend toys?

Toys as presents — giving, sharing.

Stories: *A bear called Paddington* (Michael Bond), *The red balloon* (A. Lamorisse), *Pinnocchio* (Carlo Collodi).

From Wide Range series: 'Teddy the koala' *Blue 1*, 'The boys who made aeroplanes' *Blue 4* (the story of Wilbur and Orville Wright, two young American boys who were given a tiny 'flying-machine' as a gift from their father. Made of wood, paper and twisted rubber bands, it led eventually to their designing, building and flying the first petrol-driven plane), 'The dancing doll' *Green 1*, 'Shining Moon and his toy canoe' *Green 2*, 'The red sledge', 'Helpful Teddy' *Red 1*, 'Teddy bears' *Interest 1*, 'The sky is full of kites' *New Interest 3*, 'The children's traffic park', 'Doll's town' *More Interest 1*.

Poems and rhymes:

The lost doll

I once had a sweet little doll, dears,
    The prettiest doll in the world;
Her cheeks were so red and so white, dears,
    And her hair was so charmingly curled.
But I lost my poor little doll, dears,
    As I played in the heath one day;
And I cried for more than a week, dears,
    But I never could find where she lay.

I found my poor little doll, dears,
    As I played in the heath one day;
Folks say she is terribly changed, dears,
    For her paint is all washed away,
And her arm trodden off by the cows, dears,
And her hair not the least bit curled;
Yet for old sakes' sake she is still, dears,
    The prettiest doll in the world.

Charles Kingsley

Merry-go-round

I climbed up on the merry-go-round,
    And it went round and round,
I climbed up on a big brown horse,
    And it went up and down.

Around and around
And up and down,
Around and around
And up and down.
    I sat high up
On a big brown horse
    And rode around
On the merry-go-round
    And rode around
On the merry-go-round
    I rode around
On the merry-go-round
        Around
    And round
        And
    Round.

Dorothy W. Baruch

136

Paper boats

Day by day I float my paper boats one by one
    down the running stream.
In big black letters I write my name on them
    and the name of the village where I live.
I hope that someone in some strange land
    will find them and know who I am.

Rabindranath Tagore

A swing song
        Swing, swing,
        Sing, sing,
Here's my throne, and I am a King!
        Swing, sing,
        Swing, sing,
Farewell earth, for I'm on the wing!

        Low, high,
        Here I fly,
Like a bird through sunny sky;
        Free, free,
        Over the lea,
Over the mountain, over the sea!

        Up, down,
        Up and down,
Which is the way to London town?
        Where, where?
        Up in the air,
Close your eyes, and now you are there!

        Soon, soon,
        Afternoon,
Over the sunset, over the moon;
        Far, far,
        Over the bar
Sweeping on from star to star!

        No, no,
        Low, low,
Sweeping daisies with my toe.
        Slow, slow,
        To and fro,
Slow . . .
    Slow . . .
        Slow . . .
        Slow.

William Allingham

Bedtime
Five minutes, five minutes more, please!
Let me stay five minutes more!
Can't I just finish the castle
I'm building here on the floor?
Can't I finish the story
I'm reading here in my book?
Can't I finish this bead-chain?
It almost is finished, look!
Can't I just finish this game, please?
When a game's once begun
It's a pity not to find out
Whether you've lost or won.
Can't I just stay five minutes?
Well, can't I stay just four?
Three minutes then? Two minutes?
Can't I stay ONE minute more?

Eleanor Farjeon

Also: *See-saw, Margery Daw   Ride a cock horse*

Hymns: *1* I danced in the morning
2 When a knight won his spurs in the stories of old
3 Who built the ark?
4 Thank you for the world so sweet

Music: *Teddy bear's picnic*
Debussy, *Children's corner suite, Golliwog's cakewalk, Serenade for a doll*
Mozart, *Toy symphony*
Faure, *Dolly suite*
Tchaikovsky, *Nutcracker suite*

Pictures: K. Jakobsen, *Noah's ark*
Halsband, *Jasper* (marmalade cat and ball)
Renoir, *Les parapluies* (child with hoop)
Various Athena children's posters

A final thought — It isn't always the biggest or the most expensive toy that is the best loved.

Response: To share a toy is like sharing our love.

Prayer: Father God, we thank you for our times of play
And for the people and toys we play with.

Please keep us safely through the day,
In our work and in our play.   *Amen*

66 Harvest

Ideas on theme:

Harvest — the season for reaping and gathering of grain and other foods, the crop itself or the yield from any natural product, the result of any action or effort.

Harvest Festival — service in school or church to give thanks for completion of harvest, usually with decorations of grain, fruit, vegetables. Harvest Home — festival to mark end of harvesting season.

Harvest moon — full moon nearest to autumnal equinox (about 23 September), rising at the same time for several nights, traditionally supposed to help ripen crops.

Harvesting — the workers, machinery, significance of the weather, harvest mite (parasite), harvest mouse that nests in stalks of growing grain.

Harvest of the earth in all countries (grain, fruit, vegetables), of the sea (fish), underground (gold, coal, oil).

Man's technical achievements, efforts made on behalf of others, Oxfam, etc. The using, giving, sharing, storing of harvest produce, gifts to the old and those in special need.

Stories: *Jack and the beanstalk, Treasure Island, Appleseed John* (American story about John Chapman).

God's promise to Noah: As long as the world exists, there will be a time for planting and a time for harvest. There will always be cold and heat, summer and winter, day and night. *Genesis* 8.22.

Story of Joseph: seven years of plenty, then seven of famine *Genesis* 41. Ruth and Naomi *Ruth* 2. Parable of farmer and seed *Matthew* 13.1–23. Farmer and weeds *Matthew* 13.24–30, 36–43. Trouble at harvest time – the workers in the vineyard *Matthew* 20.1–16.

Moses said to his people: 'Count seven weeks from the time that you begin to harvest the corn and then celebrate the harvest festival to honour the Lord your God by bringing him a freewill offering in proportion to the blessing he has given you. Be joyful in the Lord's presence . . .' *Deuteronomy* 16.9–11.

Feast of Tabernacles (Succoth) – eight-day Jewish harvest festival which commemorates the journey of the children of Israel through the wilderness. Temporary dwelling-places (succah) are erected in synagogues and gardens, decorated and roofed with leafy branches, flowers and fruit. Meals and other family activities take place here.

In synagogue services, offerings of a palm branch, a flowering myrtle and a willow branch are held in the right hand, and a citron fruit in the left. They symbolise God's living presence. The festival involves prayers for rain.

The Feast of Weeks (Shavuot or Pentecost) – Jewish feast to celebrate the giving of the Ten Commandments to Moses on Mount Sinai. This Pilgrim feast takes place seven weeks after Passover, and is known as the feast of the harvest and the day of the final fruit offering.

Id-Ul-Fitr or the Small Festival – a gay Muslim fast-breaking festival at the end of Ramadan. Charity is given to the poor and new clothes and pocket money to children. Festival cards are sent to distant friends.

Chinese Mid-Autumn Festival (Chung Ch'iu), also known as the Moon Festival. This resembles the western Harvest Festival, and celebrates the birthday of the moon, coinciding with the full or harvest moon. It is also known as the Moon Cake Festival, as special cakes are eaten and offered to the moon goddess. Children are allowed to stay up late and accompany their parents to vantage points, where they light lanterns and watch the moon rise before eating moon cakes and seasonal fruits. Painted effigies often show the moon goddess in the form of a Buddhist saint.

From Wide Range series: 'Johnny Appleseed' *Red 6*, 'A tin of beans' *New Interest 3*, 'A loaf of bread' *More Interest 1*.

Poems and songs:

> There was a little man,
>   The people thought him mad.
> The more he gave away,
>   The more he always had.
>   *John Bunyan*

>   *Harvest fun*
> Load of hay, load of hay;
> Make a wish and turn away. *Anon.*

Harvest year
A cherry year,
A merry year;
A pear year,
A dear year;
A plum year,
A dumb year.
                Anon.

If I were an apple
    And grew upon a tree
I think I'd fall down
    On a boy like me.
I wouldn't stay there
    Giving nobody joy,
I'd fall down at once
    And say 'Eat me, my boy.'
                        Anon.

Enough

It does not matter that my house is rather small;
One cannot sleep in more than one room!
It does not matter that I have not many horses;
One cannot ride on two horses at once!

Po Chü-i

A farmer's boy

They strolled down the lane together.
The sky was studded with stars.
They reached the gate in silence,
And he lifted down the bars.
She neither smiled nor thanked him,
Because she knew not how,
For he was just a farmer's boy
And she a Jersey cow!

Anon.

Vegetable fantasies

Oscar was a radish
  Blond and tall and slim,
All the lady radishes
  Flirted with him.
He was so proud
  He grew above them all;
But the gardener pulled him
  Because he was too tall.
The moral is here:
  Don't be too high
Or you'll get weeded out
  By and by.

Hugh was a cabbage,
  Sturdy and strong,
Who sat in the garden
  Singing a song.
He was so noisy
  The cook picked him out
From all his neighbours
  To make sauerkraut.
This is the moral
  The story would show;
The softer you sing, why
  The longer you'll grow.

H. U. Hoyt

Croptime

It is croptime
And the chimneys
Are smoking, are smoking;

And the carts,
Heavy-laden,
Are groaning, are groaning.

Little children
The sweet canes
Stand sucking, stand sucking.

While the clear juice
Down their elbows
Is dripping, is dripping.

I shall sit here
And gaze at
Kites flying, kites flying.

Will you join me?
For it's cool with
Wind blowing, wind blowing.

Vilma Dubé

141

Jamaican bananas
fresh-cut from the
tree.
Photograph: Topham

Grapes for port,
Portugal.
*Photograph: BBC Hulton
Picture Library*

See, here are red apples

1 See here are red apples for you and me,
  We eat them to make us grow strong.
  So now we are glad and say 'thank you'
    to God,
  And sing him our harvest song.

2 See, here are bananas for you and me,

3 See, here are green marrows for you and me,

4 See, here are big turnips for you and me,

5 See, oranges golden for you and me,

6 See, grapes white and purple for you and me,

7 See, loaves big and crusty for you and me,

Winifred E. Barnard

Praise

Praise the Lord for all the seasons,
  Praise him for the gentle spring,
Praise the Lord for glorious summer,
  Birds and beasts and everything.

Praise the Lord who sends the harvest,
  Praise him for the winter snows;
Praise the Lord, all ye who love him,
  Praise him, for all things he knows.
                            Mary Anderson

Hymns: *1* We plough the fields and scatter
2 Glad that I live am I
3 Morning has broken, like the first morning
4 The farmer comes to scatter the seed

Music: Beethoven, *Symphony no. 6 in F (Pastoral)*
Oats and beans and barley grow (traditional singing game)
T. C. Sterndale Bennett, *Leaning* (words by Hugh E. Wright)

Pictures: Van Gogh, *Peasant reaping, Woman gleaning, Harvest*
Lowry, *Coming from the mill*
H. Vuong, *Rice market, Banana sellers*
Sunday supper, Nature's feast (Athena)

A final thought — Give us this day our daily bread . . .

Response: God's gifts to us . . . our work . . . thank you for the
harvest!

Prayer: Bread is a lovely thing to eat —
God bless the barley and the wheat!

A lovely thing to breathe is air —
God bless the sunshine everywhere!

The earth's a lovely place to know —
God bless the folks that come and go!

Alive's a lovely thing to be —
Giver of life — we say — bless thee! *Amen*
                    H. M. Sarson, Lovely things

67   Good neighbours

Ideas on theme:

Definition of neighbour — dweller next door, same street, village or district, adjacent country. In school — neighbour in classroom, next class, other schools — linked by age, location or special interest.

Neighbourly feelings — by implication kindly or friendly. Neighbourly acts — helping those in need, either individually or as part of a group.

Good neighbours — Who needs one? Who can be one? Schemes exist whereby district organisations match local needs with offers of help. For example, a community at Broxbourne in Hertfordshire has a 'Fish Scheme' of mutual support. Although the fish is a Christian symbol, the scheme recognises no boundary and involves anyone. (Early Christians under persecution used the fish as a secret sign. The initial letters in Greek of 'Jesus Christ Son of God Saviour' spell the Greek word for fish.)

Historical and contemporary examples of those who behave in a neighbourly way, many of which can be found in newspapers and magazines. Guiding and Scouting motto of 'Lend a Hand'.

Stories: Who is my neighbour? Story of the good Samaritan *Luke* 10.25–37.

Mother Teresa — a Yugoslavian girl who became a nun and went to India. She taught in a Calcutta convent, where she became aware of the desperate needs of the sick and dying, so moved to the slum area of the city to care for them. She is the founder of the Sisters of Charity.

The wheel on the Jong — a community story about Dutch children who wanted to bring back the storks to their village (Lutterworth/Penguin).

From Wide Range series: 'The man with 60 000 children' (Dr Barnardo) *Green 5*, 'The school on wheels' *Red 5*, 'Eros' (Earl of Shaftesbury) *Blue 5*, 'At the sign of the ladybird' (Pestalozzi) *New Interest 4*, 'Part of the way' (Gladys Aylward) *New Interest 2*, 'Lady of Newgate', 'The winter of '54' (Florence Nightingale) *History 4*.

Poems:

>   *Kalu Kauwa*
>   Ladies are peculiar.
>   I'm sure you will agree
>   When I tell you how my neighbour
>   Has behaved with me.

I left a dead and tasty mouse
For her dinner Sunday night.
Would you believe she fainted –
Not from joy, but fright?
I waited till she'd recovered;
I said, 'How do you feel?'
She said, 'Go away, you nasty crow!'
And let out such a squeal!
    I felt most insulted;
    I'm sure you would have too.
    So I stopped being friendly
    For almost a week or two.
When next I went to see her,
I found to my surprise,
She'd bought herself a puppy
Of a small and ugly size.
    A lady needs a better pet
    Was all that I could say.
    So I pecked and pecked that nasty pup
    Until he ran away.
My neighbour was alone again;
I thought she'd like a chat.
But she shooed me off impolitely —
What can you say to that?
    Still, I'm generous; I forgave her.
    Next day I went again.
    I found she'd bought a parrot
    Thin, miserable and plain!
I felt sorry for the parrot
Imprisoned in a cage.
'You shouldn't be sitting idle,'
Said I, 'not at your age.'
    So I unlocked the cage door
    And watched him fly away.
    I said, 'Kalu Kauwa, good for you,
    This is your good deed for the day!'
Once my neighbour was alone
So I stopped to say hello.
I feel neighbours should be friendly,
And I'm a friendly crow.
    She was reading a newspaper;
    I hopped up to her chair.
    She just went on reading
    As if I wasn't there!

'Good morning,' I cawed cheerfully;
And it was a lovely day.
She threw her paper straight at me;
'You nuisance! Go away!'
  I didn't flinch or budge an inch,
  I just picked the paper up,
  And looking sad and dignified,
  I put it near her cup.
She laughed and said, 'You crazy crow!'
And offered me some bread.
I wanted to reject it
But accepted it instead.
  I still visit her occasionally;
  She always says hello.
  Ladies are peculiar;
  I'm glad that I'm a crow.

Anupa Lal

The people upstairs

The people upstairs all practise ballet.
Their living room is a bowling alley.
Their bedroom is full of conducted tours.
Their radio is louder than yours.
They celebrate week-ends all the week.
When they take a shower your ceilings leak.
They try to get their parties to mix
By supplying their guests with Pogo sticks,
And when their orgy at last abates,
They go to the bathroom on roller skates.
I might love the people upstairs wondrous
If instead of above us, they just lived under us.

Ogden Nash

Invocation of peace

Deep peace, pure white of the moon to you;
Deep peace, pure green of the grass to you;
Deep peace, pure brown of the earth to you;
Deep peace, pure grey of the dew to you;
Deep peace, pure blue of the sky to you!
Deep peace of the running wave to you,
Deep peace of the flowing air to you,
Deep peace of the quiet earth to you.

Fiona Macleod

Also: *Hiawatha* (Longfellow) The peace-pipe — or how Gitchie Manito taught the nations the secret of peace.
Puppy and I (A. A. Milne) See page 28.
Rabbit and Lark (James Reeves) See page 33.

Universal Declaration of Human Rights
In 1948 the United Nations adopted the following as part of its charter: '. . . All human beings are born free and equal in dignity and rights. They are endowed with reason and conscience and should act towards one another in a spirit of brotherhood.'

Proverbs: A friend in need is a friend indeed.
Kindness, like grain, increases by sowing.
Never put off until tomorrow what can be done today.

Hymns: *1* When I needed a neighbour were you there?
2 Kumbayah
3 If I had a hammer
4 The ink is black, the page is white

Music: Dvorak, *Symphony no. 9 (New world)*
Holst, *Planet suite*

Pictures: Lowry, *Station approach, Coming from the mill*
Various Athena *Peace* and *Love* posters

A final thought — Jesus said, 'Love your neighbour as you love yourself.'
Confucius taught, 'Never do to others what you would not like them to do to you.'

Response: May we be alert to the needs of our neighbours.

Prayer: *From a Canadian school creed*
This is our school,
Let peace dwell here,
Let the room be full of contentment,
Let love abide here.
Love of one another,
Love of mankind,
Love of life itself,
And love of God.
Let us remember that as many hands build a house,
So many hearts make a school.   *Amen*

Gitchie Manito with peace-pipe, from a National Theatre production of *Hiawatha*.
Photograph: Laurence Burns

68 Rainbow colours

Ideas on theme:
Rainbow — the brilliantly-coloured bow or arch seen when rain is falling opposite the sun (a similar lunar rainbow can be formed by the moon, rarely seen).

The colours of the rainbow — conventionally: red, orange, yellow, green, blue, indigo, violet. Make rainbow colours with a beam of light through a glass prism. Sequence of rain, sun, rainbow — silver linings!

How an artist uses paint colours — primary colours (red, blue, yellow), the mixing of colours, names of colours, recognition of shades, colour blindness?

Our colouring — hair, eyes, skin, of different nationalities.

Colour in nature — birds (peacock's tail), fish (rainbow trout), animals, insects (butterflies), plants (flowers), trees, etc., food (fruit, vegetables), seasonal changes (weather, sky, sea, land).

Nature's disguise — natural camouflage (chameleon), human camouflage (clothes). Colour of clothes at home and at school (uniforms, etc.). Colour in clubs, organisations, states, nations — badges, uniforms, national flags, etc. Symbolic coloured flags — black (pirate), red (danger), white (truce), yellow (warning of infection).

Colours for special occasions — sports, christenings, weddings, funerals. Histogram of favourite colours.

Use of colour in clothing and decoration (warm/cool colours), in patchwork, stained glass, kaleidoscope, etc.

Stories: The first rainbow (Noah and the ark). After the Flood, God promised Noah: 'Whenever you see a rainbow in the sky, remember that it is a sign to you that I have promised that the earth will never again be covered by a flood.' *Genesis* 9.8–17.

Joseph's beautiful coat — often called many-coloured, but in fact unusual for his time because it was a long coat, with sleeves. *Genesis* 37.3.

Little Red Riding Hood, The red balloon (A. Lamorisse), the crock of gold at the end of the rainbow (traditional).

From Wide Range series: 'The land of white elephants' *Green 3*, 'Helen in the dark' (Helen Keller) *Blue 6*.

Poems and songs:

Autumn morning
The south-west wind is blowing,
A red fox hurries by;
A lake of silver water
Reflects a rainbow sky.
                    A. White

YOU
You blue
   You red
You yellow
   You black
You white
YOU
              E. Gomringer

Colour
The world is full of colour!
   'Tis autumn once again
And leaves of gold and crimson
   Are lying in the lane.

There are brown and yellow acorns,
   Berries and scarlet haws,
Amber gorse and heather
   Purple across the moors!

Green apples in the orchard,
   Flushed by a glowing sun;
Mellow pears and brambles
   Where coloured pheasants run!

Yellow, blue and orange,
   Russet, rose and red —
A gaily-coloured pageant —
   An autumn flower bed.

Beauty of light and shadow,
   Glory of wheat and rye,
Colour of shining water
   Under a sunset sky!
                    A. White

Yellow
I like a colour that's bright and gay,
A yellow 'mac' for a rainy day.

And buttercups on a field of green
And fairy gold for a fairy queen.

I like the gold of the morning sun
Coming to tell me day has begun.

And shining softly through the night,
The yellow glow of the candle-light.
                    H. L. Black

151

Colours

What is pink? a rose is pink
By the fountain's brink.

What is blue? the sky is blue
Where the clouds float through.

What is white? a swan is white
Sailing in the light.

What is yellow? pears are yellow,
Rich and ripe and mellow.

What is green? the grass is green,
With small flowers between.

What is violet? clouds are violet
In the summer twilight.

What is orange? why, an orange,
Just an orange!

Christina Rossetti

Song to bring fair weather

You, whose day it is,
Make it beautiful.
Get out your rainbow colours
So it will be beautiful.

Nootka Indians, North America

Rainbows

It was a gloomy day,
The rain it splattered down,
   The sun came out,
   And in the sky,
A rainbow arched a crown.

It was a gloomy day
My friends had let me down.
   My mum gave me
   A hug and kiss
No need for me to frown.

   A rainbow in the sky
   A sign from heaven above,
      That God's alive,
      And cares for me
   He keeps us in his love.

Four scarlet berries

Four scarlet berries
Left upon the tree,
'Thanks,' cried the blackbird,
'These will do for me.'

He ate numbers one and two,
Then ate number three,
When he'd eaten number four,
There was none to see.

M. Vivian

Who will buy?
The old man with his bright balloons
    Is coming down the street.
The children skip to meet him
    On eager, dancing feet.
Balloons of every colour,
    Orange, blue and red,
And floating from his fingers
    Like bubbles overhead.
'Who will buy a red balloon?'
    The old man calls aloud;
'Who will buy a green balloon?'
    He asks the merry crowd.
Balloons of every colour,
    Yellow, purple, blue,
Are pulling at their long white strings —
    'Come and buy one — do!'
The old man with his bright balloons
    Has passed on up the street;
The children follow after him
    On eager, dancing feet.

L. Abney

Sayings: My heart leaps up when I behold a rainbow in the sky.
(Wordsworth)
Speech is silver — silence is golden!

Music: Beethoven, *Symphony no. 6 in F* (*Pastoral*)
Somewhere over the rainbow
Little brown jug

Pictures: Halsband, *Jasper* (marmalade cat and ball)
Durrant, *Beach scene*
Athena *Peace* and *United Nations* posters

Hymns: *1* Who built the ark?
2 He gave me eyes so I could see
3 For the beauty of the earth
4 Over the earth is a mat of green

A final thought — Seven colours in the rainbow, but countless
shades of colours surround us.

Response: The practical implications of colour to us, the beauty
and pleasure it brings to our lives.

Prayer: We thank you Father God for our colourful world. May
our eyes be quick to notice its beauty, and our hearts be thankful.

Amen

69   Cats and dogs

Ideas on theme:

Cat (*Felis catus*) — a small domesticated carnivorous quadruped. The wild cat family — lion, tiger, leopard, etc. A spiteful woman.

Dog (*Canis familiaris*) — a domesticated carnivorous quadruped. Name for male animals of dog family. A despicable fellow.

Young of cats and dogs (kittens and puppies).

Care of pets — food and drink, training, exercise, cleaning/grooming, homes (basket, kennel).

Pets' names/favourite names, histogram of class pets.

Cats' 'work' — catching mice, rats, friend/pet.

Dogs' 'work' — hunting, guard dogs, police dogs, guide dogs for the blind, hearing dogs for the deaf, mountain rescue, friend/pet.

The role of RSPCA, SSPCA, PDSA, veterinary surgeons, cat and dog homes.

Circuses, zoos, competitive shows (pedigree animals, mongrels).

'Catty' words — catfish, cat lick, catmint, catnap, cat's-cradle, cat's eye (precious stone, or reflector stud to mark traffic lanes), catfoot (ground ivy), catwalk, cattery.

'Doggy' words — dogcart, Dog Star (Sirius), dogwatch (sailors' half-watch of two hours: 4–6 pm or 6–8 pm), dog collar, doghouse, dog paddle (swimming), dog rose, dog's life, sly dog, lucky dog, sea dog, hot dog.

Cat and dog sayings — leading a dog's life, raining cats and dogs, let the cat out of the bag, like something the cat brought in, the cat's whiskers, like a cat with nine lives, like a cat on hot bricks, no room to swing a cat, not a dog's chance, like a dog's dinner, gone to the dogs, dog-in-a-manger attitude, try it on the dog, like a dog with two tails, a man's best friend is his dog.

Stories: *Orlando the marmalade cat* (Hale), *The tailor of Gloucester* (Beatrix Potter), *Dick Whittington, Puss in boots, Old Mother Hubbard, Millions of cats* (Gag), *Lassie, Madeline's rescue* (Bemelmans), *Noah, Healing of child (Matthew* 15.21–28).

From Wide Range series: 'The dog and the rice' *Blue 2,* 'Sandy the sailor dog' *Green 1,* 'The girl who sang' *Green 2,* 'Little barge girl' *Green 3,* 'The boy who loved animals' (Edwin Landseer — famous for his dog paintings and sculpted lions in Trafalgar Square), 'Dog driver' *Green 1,* 'Small story' (2) *Red 1,* 'The hotel cat' *Red 3,* 'Shaggy dog' *Red 4,* 'Karli and Kit' *Red 6,* 'Alsatians and Labradors', 'The great St Bernard Pass', 'Cats, cats, cats' *Interest 1,* 'Animals in the news' *Interest 2.*

Poems and songs:

Cat

The black cat yawns,
Opens her jaws,
Stretches her legs,
And shows her claws.

Then she gets up
And stands on four
Long stiff legs
And yawns some more.

She shows her sharp teeth,
She stretches her lip,
Her slice of a tongue
Turns up at the tip.

Lifting herself
On her delicate toes,
She arches her back
As high as it goes.

She lets herself down
With particular care,
And pads away
With her tail in the air.

M. B. Miller

Dame Trot and her cat
Sat down for to chat;
The Dame sat on this side,
And Puss sat on that.

'Puss,' says the Dame,
'Can you catch a rat,
Or a mouse in the dark?'
'Purr,' says the cat.

Anon.

My dog

His nose is short and scrubby;
  His ears hang rather low;
And he always brings the stick back,
  No matter how far you throw.

He gets spanked rather often
  For things he shouldn't do,
Like lying-on-beds, and barking,
  And eating up shoes when they're new.

He always wants to be going
  Where he isn't supposed to go.
He tracks up the house when it's raining —
  Oh, puppy, I love you so.

Marchette Chute

155

The tale of a dog and a bee

Great big dog,
Head upon his toes:
Tiny little bee
Settles on his nose.
  Great big dog
  Thinks it is a fly.
  Never says a word,
  Winks very sly.
Tiny little bee
Tickles dog's nose —
Thinks like as not
'Tis a pretty rose.

Dog smiles a smile
Winks his other eye,
Chuckles to himself
How he'll catch a fly.
  Then he makes a snap,
  Very quick and spry,
  Does his level best,
  But doesn't catch the fly.
Tiny little bee,
Alive and looking well;
Great big dog,
Mostly gone to swell.

Moral: Dear friends and children all,
  Don't be too fast and free,
  And when you catch a fly,
  Be sure it's not a bee.

Also: *The owl and the pussy-cat*
Two little kittens one stormy night (J. Taylor)
Three little kittens they lost their mittens
The song of the Jellicle Cats (T. S. Eliot)
Macavity: The mystery cat (T. S. Eliot)
I love little pussy, her coat is so warm
Hey diddle, diddle, the cat and the fiddle
Pussy-cat, pussy-cat, where have you been?
Daddy wouldn't buy me a bow-wow
One man went to mow

Sayings:

A cat may look at a king

Love me, love my dog

Help a lame dog over a stile

Every dog has his day

When the cat's away the mice
will play

Curiosity killed the cat

Put the cat among the pigeons

Barking dogs seldom bite

Let sleeping dogs lie

Give a dog a bad name and
hang him

Hymns: *1* I love God's tiny creatures
2 To God who made all lovely things
3 Who built the ark?
4 He gave me eyes so I could see

Music: Prokofiev, *Peter and the wolf*

156

Pictures: Jakobsen, *Noah's ark*
Halsband, *Jasper* (marmalade cat and ball)
Friends, Kitten (Athena)

A final thought — How much our pets depend on us for care and love.

Response: How many owners rely on their pets for guidance (the blind and deaf), for protection and for companionship.

Prayer: Dear Father God, we thank you for our pets; help us always to be kind and caring towards them. We thank you too for the animals who take care of blind or deaf people, and for all the pets who bring safety and friendship to their owners. *Amen*

---

70 Wishes

Ideas on theme:
A wish — expression of desire, or aspiration, a request, an implied command.
  Wishful thinking — belief founded on wishes rather than facts.
  Superstition — wishbone, wish on the moon, wishing cap/gate/ well, supposed to ensure wish-fulfilment.
  Who wishes what? Children — a favourite food, toy, friend. The underprivileged — food, drink, a home, a parent . . .? Adults — health, wealth, happiness, travel. Aspirations for skills — physical, intellectual, social, artistic, musical, etc.
  The realisable wish, the wish of fantasy. The realisation of wishes by luck, effort, patience. The effect of attitude (optimism/pessimism).

Stories: Any stories from the New Testament about people coming to Jesus wishing to be helped or healed. An evil wish — Herod promised to fulfil any wish of the daughter of Herodias because he was delighted by her dancing. He was forced into giving her the head of John the Baptist when asked. *Matthew* 14.3–12.
  From Wide Range series: 'The fisherman and his wife' *Blue 1* (Once a poor fisherman caught a very big fish. To his surprise the fish said he was an enchanted prince and asked to be freed. When the fisherman told his wife, she rebuked him for not demanding some reward for releasing the fish. When he went fishing again, he called the fish and repeated his wife's wishes. The fisherman went home

to find a pretty cottage instead of their old hut. Soon his wife became discontented and demanded a castle; next she asked to be Queen of all the land. Finally she went too far. When she wished to be made Lord of the Sun and the Moon their fortunes were reversed, and they found themselves back in their old hut.), 'When Anna danced' *Blue 5*, 'The boy who loved stars' *Blue 6*, 'Working for a wizard' *Green 1*, 'The lazy donkey' *Green 2*, 'The lucky nail' *Green 5*, 'The girl who loved music' *Green 6*, 'Treasure in the well' *Red 1*, 'The King's heart' *Red 3*, 'Clap hands Joanne' *Red 5*, 'Travels with Jules' *More Interest 4*.

Poems:

I keep three wishes ready

I keep three wishes ready,
Lest I should chance to meet,
Any day a fairy
Coming down the street.

I'd hate to have to stammer,
Or have to think them out,
For it's very hard to think things up
When a fairy is about.

And I'd hate to lose my wishes,
For fairies fly away,
And perhaps I'd never have a chance
On any other day.

So I keep three wishes ready,
Lest I should chance to meet,
Any day a fairy
Coming down the street.

Annette Wynne

If pigs could fly

If pigs could fly, I'd fly a pig
To foreign countries small and big —
To Italy and Spain,
To Austria, where cowbells ring,
To Germany where people sing —
And then come home again.

I'd see the Ganges and the Nile;
I'd visit Madagascar's isle,
And Persia and Peru.
People would say they'd never seen
So odd, so strange an air-machine
As that on which I flew.

Why, everyone would raise a shout
To see his trotters and his snout
    Come floating from the sky;
And I would be a famous star
Well known in countries near and far —
    If only pigs could fly!   *James Reeves*

I wish I were

I wish I were a humbug
In a little boy's pocket;
And I wish I were a lamp bulb
In a lamp socket.

    I wish I were a dustbin
    Full of odds and ends;
    And I wish I were a puppy dog
    With lots and lots of friends.

I wish I were an old boot
To be thrown at noisy cats;
I wish I were the West wind,
And could knock off people's hats.

    I wish I were a Chinese book
    Written in Peking,
    And I wish I were a bunch of keys
    Hanging on a ring.

I wish I were a mirror,
Hanging on a wall;
I wish I were so many things,
I cannot be them all.

                                    Derek Chisnall

Wishes

Said the first little chicken,
    With a queer little squirm,
'I wish I could find
    A fat little worm.'

Said the next little chicken,
    With a sharp little squeal,
'I wish I could find
    Some nice yellow meal.'

Said the third little chicken,
    With a small sigh of grief,
'I wish I could find
    A little green leaf.'

'See here,' said the mother,
    From the green garden patch,
'If you want any breakfast,
    Just come here and scratch.'

Sayings: Nothing venture, nothing win.

Practice makes perfect.

If wishes were horses, beggars would ride.

Prayer: *The prayer of the little ducks who went into the ark*
Dear God,
Give us a flood of water.
Let it rain tomorrow and always.
Give us plenty of little slugs
And other luscious things to eat.
Protect all folk who quack
And everyone who knows how to swim. *Amen*
    Carmen Bernos de Gaztold, translated by Rumer Godden

Hymns: *1* Give me joy in my heart
2 I'm very glad of God
3 Jesus' hands were kind hands
4 Stand up, clap hands, shout thank you Lord

Music: Mascagni, *Cavalleria Rusticana*
When you wish upon a star

Pictures: Heath Robinson, *How to dispense with servants,*
Aerocharribang
Friends, Earth from the moon (Athena)

A final thought — We tell God our wishes in prayer.

Response: He replies with 'Yes', 'No', or 'Wait a while'.

Prayer: We thank you Father God, for all the joys and blessings
of today. *Amen*

---

71 Questions and answers

Ideas on theme:
Question — sentence framed to elicit answers/information.
Answer — something said or done in response to a question.
    Questions — spoken, written, by actions, rhetorical questions.
Question masters, quizzes, favourite programme? Class spelling bee.
Question marks. Questions expected from children, mothers, fathers,
teachers, doctors, dentists, policemen, shopkeepers, milkmen, etc.
What answers are expected? Children's questions — at home, school,
in community.
    Answers — from people, books, films, TV, radio, experience,
instinct. Information, opinions, advice, warnings (safety, etc.).
Right/wrong, truth/lies, honesty/dishonesty (conscience).

Stories: The visit of the Queen of Sheba '. . . she travelled to Jerusalem to test him (King Solomon) with difficult questions . . .' *1 Kings* 10.1–13

'Where can wisdom be found? Where can we learn to understand? . . . God said to men, to be wise, you must worship the Lord. To understand you must turn from Evil.' *Job* 28.12–28

Jesus was asked, 'Teacher, which is the greatest commandment in the Law?' He answered: 'Love the Lord your God with all your heart, with all your soul and with all your mind. This is the greatest and the most important commandment. The second most important commandment is like the first: Love your neighbour as you love yourself.' *Matthew* 22.36–39.

Jesus in the Temple — When he was twelve, Jesus disappeared after the family visit to Jerusalem for the Passover Feast. After three days of searching they found him in the Temple with the Jewish teachers, listening to them and asking questions. His mother rebuked him, 'Son, why have you done this to us?' and he replied, 'Why did you have to look for me? Didn't you know that I had to be in my Father's house? *Luke* 2.41–50.

From Wide Range series: 'The missing boat', 'Why the sea is salt' *Blue 4*, 'What happened to the forest?' *Red 3*; Various quiz books: *Blue 1* and *6*, *Green 3* and *4*, *Red 2*, *More Interest 1, 2* and *4*, *New Interest activity books 1* and *3*.

Poems:

I keep six honest serving men
   (They taught me all I know);
Their names are WHAT and WHY and WHEN
   And HOW and WHERE and WHO.

Kipling, The serving men

I wonder

I wonder why the grass is green,
And why the wind is never seen?

Who taught the birds to build a nest,
And told the trees to take a rest?

O, when the moon is not quite round,
Where can the missing bit be found?

Who lights the stars, when they blow out,
And makes the lightning flash about?

Who paints the rainbow in the sky,
And hangs the fluffy clouds so high?

Why is it now, do you suppose,
That Dad won't tell me, if he knows?

Jeannie Kirby

Who's in?

'The door is shut fast
  And everyone's out.'
But people don't know
  What they're talking about!
Say the fly on the wall,
And the flame on the coals,

And the dog on his rug,
And the mice in their holes,
And the kitten curled up,
And the spiders that spin —
'What, everyone out?
  Why, everyone's in!'

Elizabeth Fleming

What kind of music?

What kind of music does Tom like best?
Drums and fifes and the trumpet's bray.
What kind of music does Jenny like?
A whirling waltz-tune sweet and gay.
  What music pleases Elizabeth?
  She loves a symphony solemn and grand.
  What kind of music does Benny like?
  A roaring, rhythmical ragtime band.

But the kind of music that Mary loves
Is any little gay or comical tune,
Played on a fiddle or clarinet
That skips like a leafy stream in June.

James Reeves

Who made . . .?

Who made peace?
Who made love?
Nobody else
But the One above.

Who made the sun?
Who made the moon?
Who made the object
That tells it is noon?

Who made pillows?
Who made beds?
Who made the brains
That fit in our heads?

I know who,
And you know too;
But if you don't know,
God still loves you.

Maria Gonzalez (age 8, Trinidad and Tobago)

Questions

I often wonder why, oh why,
All grown-ups say to me:
'When you are old and six foot high,
What do you want to be?'

I sometimes wonder what they'd say
If I should ask them all
What they would like to be, if they
Were six years old and small.

Raymond Wilson

Happiness?	*Only my opinion*
I feel a bit happier,	Is a caterpillar ticklish?
When I see a kingfisher	Well, it's always my belief
In the spring green willows,	That he giggles, as he wiggles
And the oak leaved ferns	Across a hairy leaf.
By the lemon wood trees.	*Monica Shannon*
Clifton R. Foster (age 11)	

Sayings: Ask no questions and you'll be told no lies.
Ask a silly question!

Hymns: *1* Can you count the stars?
2 Twinkle, twinkle little star
3 When I needed a neighbour were you there?
4 Who built the ark?

Music: Strauss, *Thunder and lightning polka*
Traditional, *Can you dance the polka?*
Who killed Cock Robin?
Oh, dear, what can the matter be?
Where are you going to, my pretty maid?

Pictures: Jakobsen, *Noah's ark, Adam and Eve*

A final thought — The path of learning?

Response: Ask, and you will receive;
seek, and you will find;
knock, and the door will be opened. *Matthew 7.7*

Prayer: Dear Father God, we ask for your blessing on our school
today, we seek to learn what is true; please guide us to do what is
right, for Jesus' sake.   *Amen*

---

72 Down comes the rain

Ideas on theme:
Rain — condensed moisture of atmosphere falling in drops of water.
   The rains — rainy season in tropical countries. Rainforest —
luxuriant tropical forest with heavy rainfall. Rain shadow — region
shielded from rain by mountains. Rainwater — pure water from rain
as distinct from springs and wells. Rainworm — common earth-
worm.

Weather forecasts — folk-lore forecasts according to signs of nature (who can smell rain?), forecasts based on scientific evidence. Rain gauge — instrument to measure rainfall.

Rainmaking — attempts to make rain fall by artificial means. Rainmaker — sorcerer who trys to produce rain by magic. Rain off/out — prevent or curtail an event by rain (especially sports fixtures). Raincheck — ticket given for later use when baseball match is interrupted by rain, promise that an offer will be maintained, though deferred. Rain words — showers, downpour, deluge, rainstorm, to rain cats and dogs.

Too much rain: floods — where likely, who affected, who helps. Too little rain: drought — water storage, rationing, wells, dams, reservoirs. Water divining. Rain needed by man for drinking, washing, cleaning, industry, farming. Rain needed by plants and animals for drinking, washing, etc.

Wet days — at school, at home, on holiday, when shopping, travelling. Raincoats, wellingtons, umbrellas, bus shelters.

Stories: Noah and the ark *Genesis* 6–8. The story of St Swithin — Swithin was a Bishop of Winchester and a very popular man, ever ready to help those in need. He travelled around the country teaching and preaching. He wished, when he died, to be buried in the fresh air. This was done, but years later when he was made a saint by the Pope, the monks decided to give him a suitable tomb in the cathedral. On the 15th of July, the date agreed to move his body, it began to rain heavily and continued for forty days and nights. Eventually the monks left his body in peace and built a little chapel over the grave.

From Wide Range series: 'The healing waters' *Blue 4*, 'Down comes the rain', 'Water tricks' *Green 4*, 'Treasure in the well' *Red 1*, 'The water of life' *Red 2*, 'Treasure under the sea' *Interest 1*, 'Artesian well' *Interest 4*, 'Well dressing' *More Interest 4*.

Poems:

Wellingtons
Wellies, wellies, wellingtons,
Wellingtons are fun,
Wear them on a rainy day
And no harm can be done.

Splish and splash and splosh and splush
Through puddles and the gutter,
Wellies keep your feet quite dry,
So mother will not mutter.

Socks will not be wringing wet,
So there should be no sneezes,
You don't catch cold with wellies on,
Or get bad coughs and wheezes.

Splish and splash and splosh and splush,
Until you see the sun,
Raw and rotten rainy days
With wellies on are fun!

Daphne Lister

Very lovely

Wouldn't it be lovely if the rain came down
'Till all the water was quite high over all the town,
If the cabs and buses all were set afloat
And we had to go to school in a little boat?

Wouldn't it be lovely if it still should pour,
And we all went up to live on the second floor.
If we saw the postman sailing up the hill
And we took the letters in, at the window sill.

It's been raining, raining, all the afternoon
All these things might happen really very soon.
If we woke tomorrow and found they had begun,
Wouldn't it be glorious, wouldn't it be fun!

Rose Fyleman

Rain in the night

Raining, raining,
All night long,
Sometimes loud, sometimes soft
Just like a song.

There'll be rivers in the gutters
And lakes along the street,
It will make our lazy kitty
Wash his dirty feet.

The roses will wear diamonds
Like Kings and Queens at court;
But the pansies get all muddy
Because they are so short.

I'll sail my boat tomorrow
In wonderful new places,
But first I'll take my watering pot
And wash the pansies' faces.

Amelia J. Burr

Rain
I opened my eyes
And looked up at the rain
And it dripped in my head
And flowed into my brain
So pardon this wild crazy thing I just said
I'm just not the same since there's rain in my head.
I step very softly
I walk very slow
I can't do a hand-stand
Or I might overflow.
And all I can hear as I lie in my bed,
Is the slishity-slosh of the rain in my head.

Shel Silverstein

Sayings:

If the oak is out before the ash,	Mackerel sky,
Then we'll only have a splash;	Mackerel sky,
If the ash is out before the oak,	Not long wet
Then we'll surely have a soak.	And not long dry.
A sunshiny shower	Rain before seven,
Won't last half an hour.	Fair by eleven.

Hymns: *1* Thank you for every good new morning
2 Who built the ark?
3 Daisies are our silver, buttercups our gold
4 To God who makes all lovely things

Music: Strauss, *Thunder and lightning polka*
Handel, *Water music*

Pictures: Michel de Gallard, *A sudden shower*
Renoir, *Les parapluies*
Heath Robinson, *Spring cleaning in Noah's ark*

A final thought — We sometimes associate tears with rain.

Response: But then the sun shines, and rainbows follow!

Prayer: Today dear Lord, we thank you for your
precious gift of rain.
However dark a storm may be, we know your
love will keep us safe,
'Till the sun breaks through, and rainbows
climb again. *Amen*

166

73 On the move

Ideas on theme:
On the move — progressing, moving about, changing position.

Development of movement — crawl, walk, run, jump, skip, hop, dance (music and movement), swim. Small movements — nod, wave, wink, shrug. Large movements — leap, spring.

Speed of movement — leisurely, hurried. Quality of movement — jerky, smooth, erratic, graceful, awkward.

In nature — movements appropriate to land animals, plants, insects, birds, fish.

On the move. By land — cycle, car, bus, train, tractor, ambulance. By sea — surfboard, canoe, raft, sailing dinghy, ship. By air — aeroplane, helicopter, balloon, parachute. Under sea — divers, submarines. Space travel — astronaut, Space Shuttle, Skylab, moon-walk, etc.

Competitive movement — dance, sports (school, professional, Olympics).

Moving house, school, and even country (use of maps, globe).

Make a move in games (chess), moving pictures, moving staircase, escalators, lifts.

Stories: Accounts of class visits, individual adventures, topical travel or sports stories. People of interest — Noah, Joseph, Moses, Solomon, Jesus, Paul, Krishna, Buddha, Muhammad, space travellers, and all explorers.

From Wide Range series: 'The coal lorry' *Blue 1*, 'The tune that flew away', 'The procession' *Blue 2*, 'The church that crossed the sea' *Blue 4*, 'The ski race', 'When Anna danced' *Blue 5*, 'The run for Oklahoma' *Blue 6*, 'Moving day for ducks' *Green 1*, 'Little barge girl' *Green 3*, 'The red sledge' *Red 1*, 'The man who wouldn't move', 'Cartwheels' *Red 3*, 'The race of Harald Gille' *Red 4*, 'The school on wheels' *Red 5*, 'Jet flight' *Red 6*, 'Aeroplane' *Interest 1*, 'Sports and sportsmen' *Interest 4*, 'Railways that climb mountains' *New Interest 1*, 'It walked one night' *New Interest 2*, 'The church that moved', 'Adrift in the Pacific' *New Interest 4*, 'Kon-Tiki' *More Interest 3*, 'The flying Finn', 'The long, long journey' *More Interest 4*, 'Towards the setting sun' *History 2*, 'The motor car man' *History 4*.

Poems:

The sewing machine

I'm faster, I'm faster than fingers,
        much faster.
No mistress can match me, no mistress
        nor master.
My bobbin is racing to feed in the
        thread,
Pink, purple, grey, green, lemon-yellow,
        or red.
My needle, my needle, my slim sharp
        steel needle,
Makes tiny, neat stitches in trousers
        and dresses,
And firmly my silver foot presses,
        it presses.
I'm fast, I'm faster than fingers,
        much faster.
        Gwenn Dunn

Slowly

Slowly the tide creeps up the sand,
Slowly the shadows cross the land.
Slowly the cart-horse pulls his mile,
Slowly the old man mounts the stile.

Slowly the hands move round the clock,
Slowly the dew dries on the dock.
Slow is the snail — but slowest of all
The green moss spreads on the old brick wall.
        James Reeves

As I put out to the open sea

As I put out
To the open sea,
With one little sail
Set over me,
   I'll not be afraid
   If the waves are tall,
   I'll say to the one
   Who made us all:
   My boat is little,
   Your sea is wide,
O God, my Father,
Be my guide.
        M. E. Rose

The song the train sang
Now
When the
Steam hisses;
Now when the
Coupling clashes;
Now
When the
Wind rushes,
Comes the slow but sudden swaying,
Every truck and carriage trying
For a smooth and better rhythm,
For a smooth and singing rhythm.

This . . . is . . . the . . . one . . .
That . . . is . . . the . . . one . . .
This is the one,
That is the one,
This is the one, that is the one,
This is the one, that is the one.

Over the river, past the mill,
Through the tunnel under the hill;
Round the corner, past the wall,
Through the wood where trees grow tall,
Then in sight of the town by the river,
Brake by the crossing where white leaves quiver.
Slow as the streets of the town slide past
As the windows stare at the jerking coaches
Coming into the station approaches.

Stop at the front.
Stop at the front.
Stop . . . at the front.
Stop . . . at the . . .
Stop.   AHHHH!   *Neil Adams*

> *Taking off*
The airplane taxies down the field
And heads into the breeze
It lifts its wheels above the ground
It skims above the trees.
It rises high and higher
Away up toward the sun
It's just a speck against the sky
   and now it's gone.
> > > *Anon.*

Kite

A kite on the ground	A kite in the air
is just paper and string	will dance and will caper
but up in the air	but back on the ground
it will dance and will sing.	is just string and paper.

Anon.

Hymns: *1* For all the strength we have
2 Hands to work and feet to run
3 I danced in the morning
4 The farmer comes to scatter the seed

Music: Wagner, *The Flying Dutchman*
Tchaikovsky, *Swan Lake*
Coates, *Sleepy lagoon*

Pictures: Tay Bak Koi, *Boats*
Jakobsen, *Noah's ark*
Lowry, *Station approaches*
Flying free, Stampeding horses (Athena)

A final thought — Movement is a vital sign of life.

Response: The quality of life is our goal.

Prayer: Father, we thank thee for the night
And for the pleasant morning light,
For rest and food and loving care
And all that makes the day so fair.
Help us to do the thing we should
To be to others kind and good,
In all we do, in all we say,
To grow more loving every day. *Amen*

---

74 Tools for work and play

Ideas on theme:
A tool can be an implement for manual work, an instrument for achieving any purpose, a person who acts as an instrument of another.

Identification of tools for specific purposes, e.g. for artists, builders, carpenters, children at play, cooks, dentists, doctors, farmers, fishermen, foresters, gardeners, housewives, jewellers, mathematicians, miners, musicians, needlewomen, sports enthusiasts, students, etc.

The learning and practice of skills — tools used by primitive man, tools for the future?

Stories: Rumpelstiltskin, The tailor of Gloucester, Pinnocchio, selected adventures from Paddington Bear stories.

From Wide Range series: 'The boy who liked engines' (George Stephenson) *Blue 2*, 'The boys who made aeroplanes' (Wilbur and Orville Wright), 'The story of clocks', 'The story of writing' *Blue 4*, 'The boy who liked music' (Mozart) *Blue 5*, 'The first cart' *Green 4*, 'The boy with ideas' (Edison) *Green 6*, 'Evonne' (tennis star), 'Jet flight' (Frank Whittle) *Red 6*, 'The writing machine' *Interest 3*, 'A far-off sound' (Bell — telephone) *Interest 4*, 'The musician' *More Interest 2*.

Tools for Self Reliance
When Glyn Roberts returned from Africa he told his mother of the desperate need for simple hand tools in the underdeveloped communities he had visited. 'How sad,' she replied, 'when in this road alone there must be at least fifteen homes where elderly people have a lifetime's store of tools they no longer need, which are probably just rusting away in the garage or garden shed.' It was this remark that led to the successful project now known as Tools for Self Reliance.

TFSR is a charity which organises the collection on a voluntary basis of hand tools, which are then sorted, cleaned and renovated, often in school and college workshops. The tools are arranged in kits and sent to development projects overseas. TFSR also aims to develop personal links of understanding and support between the groups that send and those that receive.

There is a great need for tools such as hammers, saws, chisels, and files in training centres and community workshops, where young apprentices are completing wood and metalwork courses. At one time there was a shortage of vices — one of the most important tools for a workshop. A new vice costs between £25 and £35. However, the British Steel training workshop in Hartlepool were looking for useful products for students to make. They now make vices for TFSR for the cost of materials only.

The cost of transporting the tools to underdeveloped communities has been met by various charities such as Christian Aid. The scheme has spread to other countries, including Australia, where it is known as Aid Tools. In the first three years of operation, TFSR had sent 15 000 tools to seventy-four communities, in eleven countries of Africa, Asia and South America. The tools are used to make tables, chairs, beds, window frames, doors, watering cans, stoves, carts, etc.

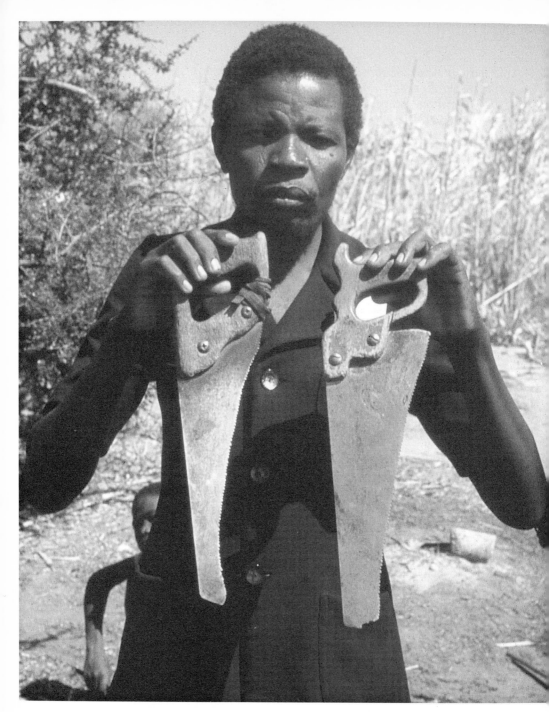

The only two saws available to a co-operative of twenty-eight men working in wood and metal at the village of Nzunguni, in Dodoma region, central Tanzania, June 1983.
Photograph: © Tools for Self Reliance

TFSR have purchased a site at Netley Marsh, near Southampton, to facilitate their work of storing, repair, sorting and crating of tools ready for despatch to the nearby docks. A permanent workshop has also been established in London, and this worthwhile project has now widened its scope to collect gardening tools and items for sewing and knitting.

(*TFSR*, *Netley Marsh Workshops*, Southampton S04 2GY)

Proverbs:

A bad workman blames his tools.

A little help is worth a lot of pity.

A stitch in time saves nine.

Actions speak louder than words.

If at first you don't succeed, try, try, try again.

Little strokes fell great oaks.

You never know what you can do until you try.

If a task is once begun
Never leave it till it's done.
Be the labour great or small
Do it well or not at all.

For want of a nail the shoe was lost,
For want of a shoe the horse was lost,
For want of a horse the rider was lost,
For want of a rider the battle was lost.

Poems:

Cobbler, cobbler
Cobbler, cobbler, mend my shoe,
Get it done by half past two;
Stitch it up, and stitch it down,
Then I'll give you half a crown.
                    Anon.

Engineers
Pistons, valves and wheels and gears
That's the life of engineers
Thumping, chunking engines going
Hissing steam and whistles blowing.

There's not a place I'd rather be
Than working round machinery
Listening to that clanking sound
Watching all the wheels go round.
                    Jimmy Garthwaite

173

The brick
The bricklayer laid a brick on the bed of cement,
Then, with a precise stroke of his trowel, spread another layer
And, without a by-your-leave, laid on another brick.
The foundations grew visibly,
The building rose, tall and strong, to shelter men.

Michel Quoist

The piano
There is a lady who plays a piano;
  She lets me listen if I keep still.
I love to watch her twinkling fingers
  Fly up and down in scale or trill.

I love to hear the great chords crashing
  And making the huge black monster roar;
I love to hear the little chords falling
  Like sleepy waves on a summer shore.

James Reeves

In this poem, Eli the silversmith has come to visit Joseph the
carpenter in his Nazareth workshop, when Jesus was just twelve
years old. Joseph is talking about Jesus.

Joseph
He's a good lad — never gives us any trouble:
Knows how to use plane and chisel,
The different feels of wood.
Since he could grasp a nail he's helped me here,
Held planks for measuring,
And watched while I fashioned yokes and ploughs.
He'll be a craftsman — he has the hands . . .
Just twelve. Next March he'll come with us
Up to Jerusalem for the Passover.
A man already — and only yesterday
I built the cradle for him.

Clive Samson

Hymns: *1* If I had a hammer
2 Who built the ark?
3 God of concrete, God of steel
4 For all the strength we have

Music: Debussy, *Children's corner suite*

Pictures: Heath Robinson, *How to dispense with servants*
Van Gogh, *Peasant reaping, Woman gleaning*
Lowry, *Coming from the mill*

A final thought — The importance of the right tool, for the right job, in the right hands.

Response: Could humour, perseverance and prayer also be regarded as tools for living?

Prayer: Dear God, please help us in our work and play, to do our best in every way. *Amen*

---

75 Gold

Ideas on theme:

Definition — a precious yellow non-rusting pliable metallic element, used as a monetary medium.

Gold as a substance — valuable, precious, brilliant, beautiful, offering wealth. As good as gold. Worth one's weight in gold.

Activities related to gold — mining, gold beating (gold leaf), goldsmith, dentistry, the sign of the three gold balls (pawnbroker).

The colour gold in nature — goldcrest, goldfinch, golden eagle, goldfish, goldsmith beetle, golden hamster, golden perch, golden chain (laburnum), golden rod (flower), goldilocks (type of buttercup). Golden: enhancing names of places — Golden Horn (Harbour of Istanbul), Golden State (California).

Gold to signify achievements/reward — gold medal for an Olympic first, gold disc for an artiste who sells a million copies of a record, golden jubilee (50th anniversary of a sovereign's accession to the throne), golden wedding (50th anniversary). Gold, the bull's eye of an archery target. Pot of gold at the rainbow's end.

Where to find gold — the search (Gold Rush), finding, claiming, sharing. People's attitude to gold — appreciation — need, greed?

Stories: Goldilocks and the three bears, Rumpelstiltskin, The Wise Men's gifts to Jesus, Jason and the Golden Fleece.

From Wide Range series: Concerning greed: 'Strawberry jam', 'The fisherman and his wife' *Blue 1*, 'Why the sea is salt' *Blue 4*. Concerning honesty: 'The jar of olives' *Blue 5*. 'Gold at Silver Grass' (when water proved more valuable than gold) *Green 6*, 'Gleam of gold' (an excavator throws up five gold Iron Age necklets) *New Interest 1*, 'The flying Finn' (The man who won six gold medals in six days) *More Interest 4*, 'The master pirate' (Drake finds gold in buried treasure) *History 3*.

Poems:

Gold

Bright, shining, rich,
That's the sign of gold.
People go over mountain, hill and river
Searching for gold.
Searching for it is like looking for
Buttercups in winter.

Kim (age 8)

Nature

We have neither Summer nor Winter
Neither Autumn nor Spring.
We have instead the days
When gold sun shines on the lush green canefields —
Magnificently.
The days when the rain beats
            like bullets on the roofs
And there is no sound but the swish of
            water in the gullies
And trees struggling in the high Jamaica winds . . .

H. D. Carberry

I'd love to be a fairy's child

Children born of fairy stock,
Never need for shirt or frock,
Never want for food or fire,
Always get their heart's desire:
Jingle pockets full of gold,
Marry when they're seven years old.
Every fairy child may keep
Two strong ponies and ten sheep;
All have houses, each his own,
Built of brick or granite stone;
They live on cherries, they run wild —
I'd love to be a fairy's child!

Robert Graves

The vulture

The vulture eats between his meals,
   And that's the reason why
He very, very rarely feels
   As well as you and I.

His eye is dull, his head is bald,
  His neck is growing thinner,
Oh! What a lesson for us all
  To only eat at dinner!
Hilaire Belloc

The chair mender
If I'd as much money as I could spend,
I never would cry, 'Old chairs to mend,
Old chairs to mend! Old chairs to mend!
I never would cry, 'Old chairs to mend.'
Anon.

Captain Kidd
This person in the gaudy clothes
Is worthy Captain Kidd.
They say he never buried gold,
I THINK PERHAPS HE DID.
R. and S. V. Benet

Sayings:
Eat an apple in the morning — gold.
  Eat an apple in the afternoon — silver.
    Eat an apple at night — lead.

Go to bed first, a golden purse;
  Go to bed second, a golden pheasant;
    Go to bed third, a golden bird!

From an anonymous contribution to a church magazine
We sing: Take my life,
      Take my silver,
        Take my gold.
But we keep: everything but our small change!

All that glisters is not gold.

If you know what you are talking about you have something more
valuable than gold and jewels. *Proverbs* 20.15

The Golden Rule
The law known as *The Golden Rule* exists in many languages.
The words vary slightly but the meaning is the same.
Christianity: Love your neighbour as yourself — do for others what
  you wish them to do for you.
Judaism: What is hateful to you, do not to your fellow man.
Islam: No one of you is a believer until he desires for his brother that
  which he desires for himself.

177

Hinduism: This is the sum of duty: do nothing to others which would cause you pain if done to you.

Buddhism: Don't hurt others in ways that you would find hurtful yourself.

Confucianism: Don't do to others what you would not have them do to you.

Taoism: Regard your neighbour's gain as your own gain, and your neighbour's loss as your own.

Hymns: *1* The golden cockerel
2 All things bright and beautiful
3 Daisies are our silver, buttercups our gold
4 I have seen the golden sunshine

Music: Strauss, *Gold and silver waltz*
Pop goes the weasel
If I were a rich man (Fiddler on the roof)
Beatles, *Money can't buy me love*
Money is the root of all evil

Pictures: Colin Paynton, *Autumn gold*
Van Gogh, *Sunflowers*

A final thought — The power of gold in wealth and beauty.

Response: Remember the advice: 'So don't store up your treasure on earth where it grows rusty and moth-eaten and thieves break in to steal. Store up your treasure in heaven, where no thieves break in to steal it. For where your treasure is so will your heart be also.' *Godspell* — from *Luke* 12.33

Prayer: We thank you Father God for all our many blessings. May we be quick to share with those in need, not only our belongings, but our time and our love. *Amen*

---

76 Time

Ideas on theme:

Definition — indefinite continuous duration regarded as dimension in which sequence of events takes place.

Time regulating our lives — alarm clock, school, transport, offices, sports events, shops, theatres, festivals. Time passing continuously, 'time flies', early, punctual, late.

Measurement of time — minutes, hours, days, weeks, months, years, centuries.

Time-pieces through history — shadow clocks, sundials, water clocks, candle-clocks, sandglasses (big and small — from a few minutes (eggtimers), quarter, half and one hour (sermon clocks), to four-hour glasses for ships' watches). First clocks — 1335, in Milan (no face or hands, but struck 24 hours). 1386, wrought-iron clock in Salisbury Cathedral (oldest British clock, struck 12 hours). Pendulums, hands, springs, clockwork, electronic (digital/quartz clocks and watches), timetables, calendars. Paper plate clocks — significant times of children's day.

Other measurements of time — four seasons, school terms, 'seven stages' of man's life, music (rhythm and note duration), greetings (good morning!). To keep time — in dancing, walking, singing.

Greenwich Mean Time (standard time) — basis of international time reckoning. Royal Observatory, Greenwich, is timekeeper to the world (quartz crystal clocks). BBC time signals received worldwide.

Study of time — past (history), present (*The Times*, etc.), future (astrology, horoscopes).

Old Father Time — time personified as an old man with scythe and hour glass.

Stories: Alice in Wonderland, Cinderella, Sleeping Beauty, The parable of the unforgiving servant *Matthew* 18.21–35.

From Wide Range series: 'The candle clock' *Blue 3*, 'Story of clocks', 'Big Ben' (facts and figures), 'What is time?' *Blue 4*, 'The ski race' *Blue 5*, 'A year and a day' *Red 4*, 'Once upon a time' *Red 6*, 'A day to remember', 'The cave of Altamira' *More Interest 2*.

Names of the months of the year
The months still keep their Roman names given over 2000 years ago.
January: named after the god *Janus* who had two faces. He looked
   forward and backward at the same time, so it was considered suitable to name the first month of the new year after him. He was
   said to carry a key and was thought of as standing at the gate of
   each year, waiting to open it.
February: named after a Roman festival called *Februa*, meaning to
   purify — therefore a festival for spiritual spring-cleaning.
March: named after the god *Mars* — fierce, strong and noisy god of
   war — a good name for a month when the wind often blows at gale
   force.
April: in Latin, *aprilis* means 'to open' — therefore the month when
   spring flowers and nature open to new life.

May: named after *Maia*, the mother of Mercury, the messenger of the gods. Maia was known as the daughter of Atlas, who held up the whole world.

June: named after *Juno*, the beautiful wife of Jupiter. The Romans thought that Juno drove a chariot drawn by peacocks.

July: named after *Julius Caesar*, Rome's great general. Until his time, the Roman year began in March, and July was known as Quintilis, meaning the fifth month. When Julius altered the calendar to make January the first month, Quintilis was unsuitable, so he renamed it after himself.

August: named after Caesar's grand-nephew, the Emperor Octavius. His name was changed to *Augustus*, meaning noble, and the eighth month was called after him.

September is the ninth month but is named from the Latin word *septem*, meaning seven. Before the calendar was altered this was the seventh month — likewise *October, November* and *December* were named after the Latin words for *eighth, ninth* and *tenth*, as appropriate to the old Roman year. With January as the first month the order changed, but their names have remained the same.

The Julian calendar was adapted by Pope Gregory XIII, and his Gregorian calendar has been used in Britain since 1752.

A West Indian year song

January	See how the waving corn-tops sweet Do bend, the bright New Year to greet!
February	The swish of the scythe rends the Febru'ry air, And silver-topp'd cane-fields are left lying bare.
March	Row upon row of brown earth will hide Brown seeds of cotton o'er many a hillside.
April	The hill-tops their bonnets of yellow display, Rustling brown leaves now carpet the way.
May	'Drink!' says the earth in a tender refrain, All nature seems glad at the sound of the rain.
June	June and the rose wait, hand in hand, To greet the brides o'er all the land.
July	The showers have gladden'd the meadowy way, Let's join the butterflies' dance and play.
August	This is the time for frolic and fun, Our holiday month has now begun.
September	Watch well the wind till September's done, The hurricane yet its course may run!

October	Juicy fruit on bunches high,
	Tempt the children passing by.
November	Bring in the harvest! Storms are o'er!
	Heav'n hath filled our garner floor!
December	The breezes know; they softly blow
	And whisper 'Peace at Christmas.'

Olga Comma Maynard

Sayings: In the beginning — God created the universe . . . *Genesis* 1

Observe the Sabbath and keep it holy (Eighth Commandment)

To everything there is a season and a time to every purpose under the heaven: A time to be born and a time to die . . . *Ecclesiastes* 3.1–8

Yesterday Where have you gone to yesterday and why did you have to go?
I've been wondering all the day and nobody seems to know.

Hugh Chesterman

Today Make me dear Lord polite and kind, to everyone I pray;
And may I ask you how you find YOURSELF, dear Lord today?

John Bannister Tabb

Tomorrow is another day.

Time and tide wait for no man.

Rhymes: What's the time Mr Wolf? (traditional playground game)

Tick tock, tick tock — goes my Daddy's big clock,
But my granny's little clock, goes: tick tock, tick tock, tick tock!

Hickory, dickory, dock, the mouse ran up the clock

Hymns: *1* At half-past three we go home to tea
2 Day by day
3 Morning has broken, like the first morning
4 God who made the earth

Music: Dvorak, *Symphony no. 9 (New world)*, *The clock carol*
Haydn, *Clock symphony*, *The minute waltz*

Pictures: Jodocus de Momper, *Four seasons*
Lowry, *Station approach*
Big Ben (Athena)

A final thought — What is time to us?

181

Response: Time is a dainty daisy,
time is an ancient oak,
time — the moments we waste in a day —
time is NOW.

Prayer: Here and now, dear Father God,
We thank you for our blessings.
Help us to see the best way
To use the time we have today. *Amen*

77 The Mary Rose

Sequence of events:

The building of the *Mary Rose* — 'from lists of the King's Ships 1525, the Marye Rosse, of the tonnage of 600 tons and the age of 14 years . . .' Named after the King's sister, Mary Tudor, the Mary Rose was a purpose-built warship — 'the flower of King Henry VIII's fleet'. In 1536 the ship was rebuilt at Portsmouth, and upgraded to 700 tons.

19th July, 1545 — 235 French ships lay off the Isle of Wight, ready to attack. The English fleet sailed out to meet them, but the *Mary Rose* capsized. Nearly 700 men perished within sight and sound of shore, as the nets intended to protect her from boarding by French soldiers prevented her crew from escaping. Why did she sink? Mishandling by the crew, overloading of men and guns, water rushing in through open gun ports . . .?

Salvage attempts: 16th century — The Tudors employed Venetian professionals who used ropes, pulleys, rising tides, but all raising attempts failed. Some items were salvaged.

1836 — John and Charles Deane, pioneers of helmet diving, brought many items to the surface. Most were sold at auction in Portsmouth.

1965 — The search for the *Mary Rose* began again when Alexander McKee, a Portsmouth historian, initiated Project Solent Ships.

1966 — An 1841 chart, found in Hydrographer's Department of the Royal Navy, had a red cross marking the spot where the Deane brothers had discovered the *Mary Rose*. Corresponding mounds and depressions were found on the seabed.

1967 — A sonar survey confirmed the site. The Mary Rose Committee was formed to obtain legal protection for the wreck.

1968 — A sub-mud sonar survey carried out. The committee acquired a lease from Crown Estate Commissioners, so plunderers could now be prosecuted for trespass.

1970 — The discovery of a wrought-iron breechloading gun proved identity of *Mary Rose*.

1971–1979 — The excavation continued. *1975* — The first of many dives by HRH Prince Charles.

1979 — The Mary Rose Trust formed, with Prince Charles as President. The aims are 'To find, to record, to excavate, raise, bring ashore, preserve, report on and display for all time in Portsmouth the *Mary Rose*. Also to establish, equip and maintain a museum in Portsmouth to house the *Mary Rose* . . . all for the education and benefit of the nation.'

1982 — National Maritime Year — On Monday the 11th of October the *Mary Rose* was raised and taken into Portsmouth Harbour.

The only known contemporary representation of the Mary Rose, painted in watercolour in the margin of the Anthony Roll – an inventory of Henry VIII's ships published in 1546 by a civil servant, Sir Anthony Anthony.
Photograph reproduced by permission of the Master and Fellows, Magdalene College, Cambridge

Ideas on theme:

The people of the *Mary Rose* — those who built her, those who sailed in her as a successful warship, those who died in the disaster, those who tried to salvage her.

The twentieth-century team — Alexander McKee (historian), Richard Harrison (Trust Executive Director), Margaret Rule (Archaeological Director), small full-time and part-time staff, hundreds of volunteer workers, including divers from all over the world, professional experts whose skills are needed to find, salvage, and raise the *Mary Rose* and bring her into harbour, fund raisers, shore workers, researchers, conservationists, and those who for years to come will be involved with this historic project.

The treasures revealed by the *Mary Rose*, 'a Tudor time-capsule' — over 10 000 objects recovered prior to raising of the hull, including hundreds of bows and arrows, many guns and other weapons, naval navigational equipment, rigging, carpentry tools, etc. Items from the Barber Surgeon's cabin — ointment jars, medicine bottles, syringes, operating instruments. From the Priest's cabin — a rosary, remains of wooden-covered Bible. Coins — Gold Angels (a day's pay for an admiral, five weeks' pay for a mariner). Musical instruments (including a unique shawm), pocket sundials, clothing, footwear, combs, thimbles, other personal items. Gaming board and dominoes, cooking and eating utensils, remains of last meal, oak leaf pressed between deck planks, and of course the crew's skeletons.

Conservation — contents and hull of the *Mary Rose* were preserved by a casing of mud below and fine silt above. Once salvaged, expert advice was needed to conserve all objects found. Methods varied with material of manufacture — wood, leather, textiles, iron, rope, pottery, glass.

Cost of the project? The world's most ambitious underwater archaeological exploration was estimated to cost over four million pounds. Gifts were received from individuals, organisations, local authorities, industry, business. Valuable equipment given or loaned, with supporting expertise, from outside organisations, HM services.

Story: The raising of the Mary Rose

On Saturday the 9th of October, 1982, the hull of the *Mary Rose* lay submerged and suspended from a massive steel frame, held up by the floating crane *Tog Mor*. The name is Gaelic for *Big Lifter*. A nine-hour operation began. The frame was to be lowered onto a padded cradle. During the delicate operation one leg of the frame buckled, making it impossible for the leg to enter the conical joint on the cradle.

Preparing to photograph the sterncastle of the Mary Rose using a
calibrated three-dimensional scale, during salvage operations.
Photograph: © *The Mary Rose Trust*

On Sunday the 10th of October engineers cut away the damaged leg with a thermic lance. The world waited! A small armada of boats surrounded the area in the Solent, and spectators waited on shore at Southsea and the Isle of Wight. Prince Charles arrived and dived to inspect the work. Steel cables were attached to the giant hook which supported the frame, to prevent it crushing the *Mary Rose*. The lift was unavoidably delayed and work continued throughout the night.

On Monday the 11th of October, at 8.00 am, lights shone from Tog Mor, watched by the world's reporters and TV cameras. It was raining with a gentle force 2 breeze, although gales were forecast later. The *Mary Rose* staff were on the diving vessel *Sleipner*. Margaret Rule greeted Prince Charles and King Constantine who arrived by launch at 8.05 am. After some discussion the Royal guests transferred to *Tog Mor*, crossing her decks to enter the control cabin. The Royal Standard flew, and windscreen wipers swung across the cabin windows of the giant crane. Divers were busy. *Mary Rose* divers in their red suits and yellow helmets, and Royal Engineers' divers in black suits, lowered pumps like small Daleks into the frame. Helicopters buzzed noisily overhead.

At 8.35 am all was going well. The lift was underway, and ten minutes later the yellow frame broke the surface of the Solent waters. The divers released air trapped inside the frame and secured the pumps. It was essential that water from the hull was pumped out quickly to lighten the weight.

At 9.03 am the *Mary Rose* surfaced to a greeting of sirens, hooters and a gun salute. It was the first sighting for 437 years. Within ten minutes the shape of the hull could be made out. There were congratulations, tears, champagne, cheers. The master of *Tog Mor* and his computer controlled the slow lift. The routines were repeated: raise, empty, check . . .

At 11.30 am Prince Charles, King Constantine, Margaret Rule and others boarded a jet-propelled, military combat support boat to inspect the *Mary Rose* in her cradle. The weather brightened — the forecast gale still hadn't arrived. The wreck lay cushioned on giant air-bags.

At 11.53 am there was a sudden crashing sound as the top of the frame collapsed on the *Mary Rose* in her cradle. There was a stunned silence, but the BBC commentator recovered quickly! Engineers rushed to inspect the *Mary Rose*, and indicated that no damage was apparent. The lift continued.

The sun had begun to shine by 1.00 pm, and the hull of the *Mary Rose* was above water. With dismay Margaret Rule noticed a twisted cable, but by 1.23 pm the cradle was completely clear of the water and the waiting raft barge was called in. As divers left the water to climb on *Tog Mor*, three cheers rang out. Tugs worked to position the barge under the suspended *Mary Rose*. By 2.12 pm the wreck was positioned over the barge, but the descent to the platform-deck was to prove almost as delicate as the lifting operation. It was nearly an hour before the *Mary Rose* rested on the barge in her cradle.

By 10.00 pm the *Mary Rose* had at last reached Portsmouth Harbour, to be welcomed by sirens, hooters, fireworks and the cheers of thousands of well-wishers. The next phase of the project could begin.

Hymns: *1* The sun that shines across the sea
2 When a knight won his spurs in the stories of old
3 God of concrete, God of steel
4 When lamps are lighted in the town

Music: Alison Hedger, *The Mary Rose*
Mendelssohn, *Hebrides overture*
Rimsky-Korsakov, *The sea, Sinbad's ship*
Sea shanties

Pictures: Holbein, *King Henry VIII's presentation of Charter to the Guild of Barber Surgeons*
The symbol of the Mary Rose
Illustrations of *Mary Rose Trust*, Old Bond Store, Portsmouth

A final thought — Failure — the tragic disaster in 1545.

Response: Success in 1982 — the reward for great dedication and effort by so many.

Prayer: Dear Father God, we remember all those who work or travel on the sea, and ask you to bless them and protect them from all dangers. *Amen*

78 The Sue Ryder Foundation

Ideas on theme:
Sue Ryder Foundation — 'Living Memorial' to the millions who gave their lives during two World Wars in defence of human values, to countless others who are suffering and dying today as a result of persecution.

An international Foundation — devoted to relief of suffering on the widest scale, gives personal service to those in need, affection to those who are unloved, regardless of age, race or creed, as part of the family of man.

The work — seek out and face the reality of human suffering and do something about it.

Headquarters at Cavendish, Suffolk. Also Museum (depicts work and history of the Foundation), The Home for Sick and Disabled.

Sue Ryder Homes in the UK, Europe, India. Who builds them? Who lives in them? The holiday scheme (Stagenhoe House, in Hertfordshire).

Who pays for the work? — fund raising, gifts from individuals, schools, organisations, industry. Shops, coffee-rooms, concerts and concert tours, auctions, magazines, Christmas cards, TV appeals, etc.

Who has been helped by the Sue Ryder Foundation? — Well over 250 000 children and adults of fifty nationalities.

The Foundation symbol — rosemary, for remembrance.

Story: *And the morrow is theirs* (Burleigh Press) — autobiography of Lady Ryder, CMG, OBE. Some highlights of the story:

Sue Ryder was born on the 3rd of July 1923, in Leeds, Yorkshire. Her mother had four older children, and her father had five by a previous marriage. Sue Ryder was blessed with a comfortable home and loving, talented parents. The family lived near terrible slums, so she became aware of poverty and deprivation. She was taught to care about people living in these conditions and to offer assistance.

During a stay in hospital for an operation she grew to love the doctors and nurses. After she came home she and her friends played hospitals — they gowned, scrubbed up, and masked themselves for pretend operations. Sue Ryder grew up leading a full and busy life. At eight years of age she learned to help in the dairy, and even had her own small herd of cows. When she was twelve, she attended her first school as a weekly boarder.

In the Second World War Sue Ryder volunteered to join the First Aid Nursing Yeomanry. After her period of training she was attached to a unit of the Special Operations Executive. The SOE agents were affectionately known as The Bods. Their task was top secret and very dangerous. They were trained to carry out resistance work in occupied countries. Amongst many duties, the first aid workers drove The Bods on the first stage of their missions, along country lanes to waiting aircraft on some quiet airfield runway. They also prepared flasks of coffee, sandwiches, sometimes a haybox meal, and had to check that no clues were left on the agents' clothing, which could identify them if they were caught. These agents, some from Poland, were their companions and friends. Many of them died — including Sue Ryder's best friend. She shared their fears, thoughts, and plans for the future. She recognised their courage, tolerance, faith and gaiety. Remembering these qualities, Sue Ryder realised that no plaque or monument would be enough to perpetuate their memory. Much better to go out to the sick and needy and give assistance and comfort as a 'Living Memorial'. She was sent to serve overseas and experienced personally the horrors of war.

Sue Ryder was twenty-two when the war ended, and acutely aware of our responsibility towards the dead, and of the future. After the war she worked for international relief agencies for a time, then continued on her own with some small financial help, mostly raised by her mother's efforts. She worked in bombed ruins and in hospitals and prisons, until returning home on leave in 1951. She then registered the 'Living Memorial' with the Charity Commissioners, and the Sue Ryder Foundation was born. Eventually headquarters were established at Cavendish, and support grew from a variety of sources, as the national press took an interest in the Foundation. Sue Ryder Homes were built in many places in Britain and abroad. Despite almost overwhelming difficulties, the needs of those who suffered were being recognised. Something was being done about it!

In February 1955 Sue Ryder accepted an invitation from Leonard Cheshire to visit his new Home for the Disabled at Ampthill. Neither was fully aware of the work and achievements of the other. Leonard Cheshire had distinguished himself in wartime Bomber Command of the Royal Air Force. He had been awarded the VC, the DSO three times, and the Distinguished Flying Cross. He had also been one of the two British observers at the dropping of the atom bomb on Nagasaki. The meeting of Sue Ryder and Leonard Cheshire was the beginning of a friendship, which eventually led to their marriage. Both were determined that their work should continue, but together they were strengthened and joint ventures were undertaken. Their two children Jeremy and Elizabeth were born at Cavendish, and the family live there still. The work to which they are both dedicated continues — the Living Memorial.

The Order of Smile: This award originated in Warsaw in 1967, for people who 'bestowed joy upon children'. It was the personal concept of one small boy, who also decided on its name.

The Order of Smile recently became an international award, and is known as the only Order in the world given exclusively by children to adults. Nominations are submitted by children, who list the qualities of the nominee and why he or she merits the award.

The *Order of Smile* medal, reproduced by permission of
Lady Ryder of Warsaw, CMG, OBE.

In 1980 the children at the Polish School in London, and other
children in different parts of Poland, proposed that Sue Ryder should
receive the Order of Smile, and the award was granted later that year.

A rose called Sue Ryder: A famous rose grower has propagated a
new rose named after the Founder. It is two-toned — the petals are
amber yellow on the outside and salmon on the inside.

Thoughts: The words of Doctor Karel Fleischmann, which in-
spired Sue Ryder: (He died in the gas chambers of Auschwitz.)

'One of us
Will teach these children how to sing again
To write on paper with a pencil,
To do sums and multiply:
One of us
Is sure to survive.'

. . . and the message of encouragement from an eighty-year-old
Polish lady:
'I always try to forget all the sadness . . . Always remember, keep
in top form.'

Isn't it strange that Princes and Kings
And clowns that caper in sawdust rings
And ordinary folk like you and me
Are builders of eternity.

To each is given a bag of tools,
An hour-glass and a book of rules,
And each must build, 'ere his time is flown
A stumbling block or a stepping stone.

Sue Ryder

Hymns:　*1* Father hear the prayer we offer
2 God is working his purpose out
3 The family of man
4 When I needed a neighbour were you there?

Music:　Sir Cecil Spring-Rice, *I vow to thee my country*
The music of Benjamin Britten and Peter Peers — both of whom
gave concert performances for the Foundation.
Rachmaninov, *Rhapsody on a theme of Paganini*
Brahms, *Violin concerto*
(The last two pieces were enjoyed by Sue Ryder, before she went
overseas on service with the FANY)

Pictures:　Illustrations from Sue Ryder's autobiography, *And the
morrow is theirs*

A final thought — The challenge quoted by the Foundation:

For the cause that lacks assistance,
For the wrong that needs resistance,
For the future in the distance,
And the good that I can do.

George Linnaeus Banks

Response:　Perhaps we might all live more simply, so that others
may simply live.

Prayer:　God be in my head,
　　And in my understanding;
God be in mine eyes
　　And in my looking;
God be in my mouth
　　And in my speaking;
God be in my heart
　　And in my thinking;
God be at my end,
　　And at my departing. *The knight's prayer*

79 Festivals

Ideas on theme:
Festival — a feast day, celebration, merry-making, periodic musical performance of special importance, occasion when a community celebrates something which is important and meaningful to it.

Family celebrations — birthdays, anniversaries.

School celebrations — Founders' Day, Sports Day, end of term.

Community celebrations — anniversaries. For scouts and guides — Thinking Day. Music and arts festivals — Edinburgh Festival, etc.

National celebrations — Commonwealth Day, Remembrance Sunday, Guy Fawkes Day, May Day, American Independence Day.

How do we celebrate? Many events have their own traditional forms of celebration:

With special food and drink for the occasion — Christmas dinner, pancakes, Easter eggs, hot cross buns. The Jewish traditional meal 'Seder', with symbolic dishes and ritual. Feasting/fasting.

With gifts — greetings cards, presents, sweets. Giving/receiving/thanking.

With special clothes or costumes to suit the event — Easter bonnets, fancy dress, national costumes, ceremonial dress, masks.

With music — singing, musical instruments/groups/bands/orchestras. Dance (formal or spontaneous), maypole dancing, drama.

With lights — candles, bonfires, illuminations, fireworks.

With fire, with water — as for Holi (Hindu/Sikh Festival).

With rituals — religious services/thought/prayer, processions, carnivals, parties.

With decorations — home, school, buildings. Evergreens, lights, flags.

> Why do we have a festival?
> To welcome the new, say goodbye to the old?
> To follow tradition?
> Or remind everyone —
> There's a time to be happy, a time to have fun!

This is the day that the Lord has given, we will rejoice and be glad in it! *Psalm* 118.24

Religious Festivals:
For Christians: Advent (start of Christian year, preparation for Christmas), All Saints' Day, Candlemas, Christian Aid Week, Christmas, Corpus Christi, Easter, Epiphany, Harvest, Lent,

Maundy Thursday, Mothering Sunday, Palm Sunday, days of: St
Andrew, St David, St George, St Patrick, Shrove Tuesday, Whitsun.
For Jews: Feast of Weeks, Feast of Tabernacles, Hanukkah, New
Year for Trees, Passover, Purim, Rosh Hashanah, Simchath Torah,
Yom Kippur.
For Hindus: Diwali, Durga Puja, Dusshera, Holi, Janam Ashtami,
Raksha Bandhan, Shiva Ratri, Sri Ramakrishna's Birthday.
For Muslims: Farewell Friday, Day of Hijrah, Id-Ul-Adha, Id-Ul-
Fitr, Lailat-Ul-Bara'h, Lailat-Ul-Qadr, Lailat-Ul-Isra, Wal Mi'Raj,
Muhammad's Birthday, Ramadan.
For Sikhs: Baisakhi, Diwali, Guru Gobind Singh, Guru Nanak
(Birthday), Holi.
For Buddhists: Bodhi Day, Dammacakka Day, Obon, Poson,
Veshakha Puja . . .
Dates of religious festivals: Most religions have their own calendars,
some are based on the moon and begin in spring or autumn. They
are unrelated to the Gregorian calendar, which begins on the 1st of
January and is used in most countries to date everyday events. A
Calendar of Religious Festivals (July to July) is published annually by
the Commission for Racial Equality, Elliot House, 10/12 Allington
Street, London SW1E 5EH.

Stories: Stories from the scriptures relevant to festivals being
celebrated or considered.
Festival time, by Swarn Khandpur (India Book House).
From Wide Range series: 'The first Christmas' *Green 1*, 'The
Christmas tree' (poem) *Red 1*, 'Easter Day' *Interest 2*, 'Blessing the
boats' *New Interest 2*.

Poems:

A giant's cake
Each year I have a birthday,
    When people buy me toys,
And mother gives a party
    To lots of girls and boys.

I have a cake with candles,
    And icing, pink and white,
With rosy candles lighted,
    It makes a lovely sight.

Each year the cake grows larger,
    Another light to take,
So if I grow much older
    I'll need a giant's cake.
                        E. S. Garde

At Easter

I think that Easter bunnies
  Are lots and lots of fun,
And I like candy Easter eggs —
  Every coloured one!

I like tiny Easter chicks
  And downy ducklings, too,
And so-tall Easter lilies,
  And flowers of every hue.

I like my brand-new Easter dress
  With lace and ribbons on it,
And, oh, I like especially
  My little Easter bonnet!

But better than the Easter eggs
  Or nests that bunnies hide,
Is the happy Easter feeling
  I have in my inside.

L. Abney

The Lord's name be praised
Hey, all you children,
  Bless you the Lord!
All fathers and mothers,
  Sisters and brothers,
Praise him and magnify him for ever!

All you deeps of the ocean,
  Bless you the Lord!
All whales and porpoises,
  Turtles and tortoises,
Praise him and magnify him for ever!

All field mice and larder mice,
  Bless you the Lord!
All hedgehogs and moles,
  Rabbits and voles,
Praise him and magnify him for ever!

Let everything that hath life
  Praise the Lord!

Anon.

Hymns: *1* Give me joy in my heart
2 Go tell it to the mountains
3 Praise him, praise him
4 Stand up, clap hands, shout thank you Lord
5 The ink is black, the page is white

Music: Mozart, *Coronation mass in C, Zadok the priest, Belshazzar's feast*
Saint-Saëns, *Carnival of the animals*
Sir Cecil Spring-Rice, *I vow to thee my country*
Louis Armstrong, *What a wonderful world*
Christmas carols
Negro spirituals

A final thought — The richness of our lives as we become aware of our cultural heritage. The recurring festivals and celebrations bring a rhythm and pattern to life, and in some respects a means for measuring progress.

Response: The need to respect the various minority groups in our multi-racial society.

Prayer: Dear God, we praise and thank you for the happy days of celebration and for all our many blessings.   *Amen*

80   Christmas

Ideas on theme:

The Christian festival — Advent (beginning of Christian year), Christmas Day, Epiphany (associated with coming of the Wise Men). Celebrated with church services, carols, nativity plays, music. Churches decorated with lights, winter greenery, crib.

The historical significance — derivation of 'Christmas', 'Jesus', 'X' in Xmas. Origin of the 25th of December as Christmas Day. Tradition of holly, ivy, mistletoe.

Customs — use of Advent calendars, preparation of traditional food, decoration of home, school, community, giving of cards, gifts. The tree in Trafalgar Square from the Norwegian to the British people. Traditions in other lands.

Special events — parties, pantomimes, circus, nativity plays, carol singing.

School programmes for children and guests — Christmas story with drama, mime, readings, carols, tableaux. A pageant of winter, light, colour, fire — using poetry, art, music, song, leading to nativity tableau.

Use of symbols — a Christmas star (six-pointed star of David), a Jewish seven-branched candlestick, a Christmas alphabet, to focus on various aspects of the Christmas theme.

Stories: The nativity story: *Matthew* 1.18–24, 2.1–12, *Luke* 1.26–38, 2.1–20.

Babouschka, Legend of the Christmas rose, St Nicholas the patron saint of children, The first Christmas tree, Peter Pan, Angels and shepherds (*Book of Witnesses*, David Kossof), St Francis at Greccio (the first crib), The Friston crib (a baby found in a church crib), Franz Gruber and 'Silent night'.

From Wide Range series: 'Stories of Phineas Barnum' (circus) *Blue 6*, 'The first Christmas' *Green 1*, 'The Christmas cuckoo' *Green 3*, 'Santa Claus' *Interest 2*, 'Christmas cribs' *New Interest 1*, 'The Bethlehem' *New Interest 4*.

Christmas poems and songs:

> Winds thro' the olive trees
>   Softly did blow,
> Round little Bethlehem
>   Long, long ago.
>
> Sheep on the hillside lay,
>   Whiter than snow;
> Shepherds were watching them,
>   Long, long ago.
>
> Then from the happy sky,
>   Angels bent low,
> Singing their songs of joy,
>   Long, long ago.
>
> For in a manger bed
>   Cradled, we know,
> Christ came to Bethlehem,
>   Long, long ago.
>   *Anon.*

> Why do the bells of Christmas ring?
> Why do little children sing?
>
> Once a lovely shining star,
> Seen by shepherds from afar,
> Gently moved until its light
> Made a manger's cradle bright.
>
> There a darling baby lay,
> Pillowed soft upon the hay,
> And its Mother sung and smiled:
> 'This is Christ, the holy Child!'
>
> Therefore bells for Christmas ring,
> Therefore little children sing.
>   *Eugene Field*

Nativity
I can't hear the angels —
The bombs roar and slay:
  Somewhere a baby
  Is wounded and crying,
  And somewhere a baby is crying.

I don't need to look for
A stable today:
  Somewhere the homeless
  Are searching and trying,
  And somewhere a baby is crying.

I can't see the manger —
The feast's in the way:
  Somewhere the people
  Are hungry and dying,
  And somewhere a baby is crying.
                    Cecily Taylor

Christmas

My goodness, my goodness,
It's Christmas again.
The bells are all ringing.
I do not know when
I've been so excited.
The tree is all fixed,
The candles are lighted
The pudding is mixed.

The wreath's on the door
And the carols are sung,
The presents are wrapped
And the holly is hung.
The turkey is sitting
All safe in its pan,
And I am behaving
As calm as I can!
                    Marchette Chute

Pudding charms
Our Christmas pudding was made in November,
All they put in, I quite well remember:
Currants and raisins, and sugar and spice,
Orange peel, lemon peel — everything nice
Mixed up together, and put in a pan.
'When you've stirred it,' said Mother, 'as much as you can,
We'll cover it over, that nothing may spoil it,
And then, in the saucepan, tomorrow we'll boil it.'
That night, when we children were all fast asleep,
A real fairy godmother came crip-a-creep!

She wore a red cloak, and a tall steeple hat
(Though nobody saw her but Tinker, the cat!)
And out of her pocket a thimble she drew,
A button of silver, a silver horse-shoe,
And, whisp'ring a charm, in the pudding pan popped them,

And flew up the chimney directly she dropped them;
And even old Tinker pretended he slept
(With Tinker a secret is sure to be kept!)
So nobody knew, until Christmas came round,
And there, in the pudding, these treasures we found.

Charlotte Druitt Cole

Ten little Christmas trees
Ten little Christmas trees a-growing in a line.
  The first went to Bedfordshire,
  And that left only nine.

Nine little Christmas trees all found it long to wait,
  The second went to Monmouthshire,
  And that left only eight.

Eight little Christmas trees said, 'Christmas will be heaven.'
  The third went to London Town,
  And that left only seven.

Seven little Christmas trees, and all as straight as sticks!
  The fourth went to Oxfordshire,
  And that left only six.

Six little Christmas trees, all growing and alive!
  The fifth went to Lancashire,
  And that left only five.

Five little Christmas trees said, 'Will they want some more?'
  The sixth went to Devonshire,
  And that left only four.

Four little Christmas trees, as sturdy as could be!
  The seventh went to Scilly Isles,
  And that left only three.

Three little Christmas trees all grew and grew and grew,
  The eighth went to Middlesex,
  And that left only two.

Two little Christmas trees, December almost done!
  The ninth went to Timbuctoo,
  And that left only one.

One little Christmas tree, feeling very small!
  She came to our school,
  And that was best of all.

Ten little Christmas trees, with Christmas drawing near,
  Wish you love and gladness
  And a Happy New Year.

Rodney Bennett

A Christmas wish
To every hearth a little fire,
To every board a little feast,
To every heart a joy,
To every child a toy,
Shelter for bird and beast.

Rose Fyleman

Pictures: Leonardo Da Vinci, *Virgin and child*
Many other suitable pictures available from Athena, SPCK book-shops or Oxfam.

Music: Mozart, *German dances 74–76* (Musical sleigh ride)
Tchaikovsky, *Nutcracker suite* (The Christmas scene, Journey through the snow, Waltz of the snowflakes)
Carols: *World of Christmas*, Volumes 1 and 2
See also pages 200–205.

A final thought — Christmas is the season of expectancy, prep-aration, excitement.

Response: Why do the bells of Christmas ring and little children sing? The response of an eleven-year-old boy was:
'But this is a most important day;
It's not just presents, and be gay;
It's Christ we have to celebrate,
Learning to love the folk we hate.'

J. Wellard

THEREFORE wonder, joy, goodwill.

Prayer: We thank you Father God for all the joys and happiness we share at Christmas. Especially we thank you for Jesus, your son, as we remember his birthday. *Amen*

THE SEARCH FOR LODGING

Pedida de la Posada
FLINTSHIRE

Mexican carol

Joseph 1.Lodg-ing I beg you, good man in the name of hea-ven:

My wife is wea-ry; She says She can go no far-ther,

Long have we trav-elled; have mer-cy on us good man!

God will re-ward you if you will give shel-ter to Her.

Innkeeper	2	There is no room in this place for any stranger I do not know you; be gone; and all talking cease! I do not care if great distance you have come All of your pleading is vain, so go away; let us have our peace!
Joseph	3	Listen, I beg you, for She is not a stranger; Her name is Mary, and She is the Queen of Heaven My name is Joseph; we journey from Nazareth She has been chosen by God to bear His Son, the King of Men!
Innkeeper	4	Pardon, good Joseph, for I did not know you, My house is honoured by you and the Holy Presence Great is my joy if you choose to rest here, Enter I beg you and bless this humble home; bring it happiness.
Joseph	5	Enter sweet Mary, for we now have found lodging Here is a man who to us opens home and heart. To him and all who shall thus His Son receive God shall reward with great love. Happiness He gives shall ne'er depart.

English version from the Spanish by Ruth Heller

BEHOLD THAT STAR

LANCASHIRE

U.S.A. Negro

202

2 The wise men came on from the East,
   This is the star . . .
The worship Him, the Prince of Peace.
   This is the star . . .
   Behold that star! (etc.)

3 A song broke forth upon the night,
   This is the star . . .
From angel hosts all robed in white.
   This is the star . . .
   Behold that star!
                        Thomas W. Talley

SLEEP BABY JESUS

for unison (top line only) or 2-part choir
and piano

Words by
RUZENA WOOD

Based on the folk tune
Du liegst mir im Herz
from Ludwig Erk's
Deutscher Liederschatz (c. 1870
Arranged by RUZENA WOOD

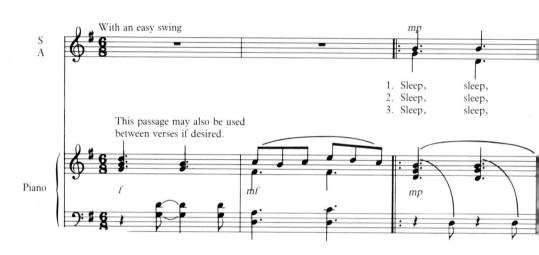

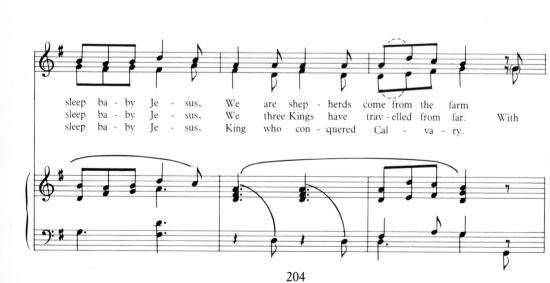

1. sleep ba - by Je - sus, We are shep - herds come from the farm
2. sleep ba - by Je - sus, We three Kings have trav - elled from far. With
3. sleep ba - by Je - sus, King who con - quered Cal - va - ry.

(' Verses 2 & 3)

Bring - ing you a fine wool -len blan - ket, flee - cy and co - sy and
gold and myrrh and frank - in - cense We foll-owed the light of a
Stay, and keep us safe in Your love And bless us this Christ - mas

p teneramente

ossia

warm. We will sing a
star. We will sing a
Day. We will sing a

p teneramente

lull - a - by Un - der the Beth - le - hem sky.

205

Index of poems

Songs with music

Subject index

Class assembly themes are asterisked.

Advent 122, 192, 195
Aeroplanes 135
African/Caribbean story 43
Allah 115
Alphabet 49
  Braille alphabet 19
Archaeology 76, 182
Asthma 5
Astronaut 90
Autumn 29, 31
Autumn term assemblies 1

*Babies 125
Bears 20, 24, 93
Bethlehem 40, 54
Birds 80, 100
Birthdays 2
Blessings 50
Blindness 17, 57
Blue Peter 88
Bonfires 14
Braille, Louis 17
Brer Anansi 43
Buddha 83, 111
Buddhist festivals 193
Busy 1, 59

Calendar 179
Canadian stories 93
Canal lock 10
*Cats and dogs 26, 154
Census 52
Centurion, Roman 55
Chinese festivals 140
Christian festivals 192, 195
*Christmas 39, 195
*Class assemblies 120
Clocks 178
*Colours 150, 175
Commission for Racial
    Equality 193

Counting 52
Courage 2, 62, 84, 86

Daedalus and Icarus 122
Danger 20
David and Goliath 32, 62
*Day and night 1, 122
Deacon, Joey 88
Disability 5, 7, 17, 26, 84, 88
Discontentment 56
Dogs for the deaf 26, 154
Dürer, Albert 132

Easter 76
Elephant 57
End of school year 118
Everyday things 16

Faith 90
Families 125, 128, 131
Farming 59
Father Christmas 66, 196
Fear 90
Feast of Tabernacles 139, 193
Feast of Weeks 140, 193
*Festivals 65, 139, 192, 195
Fighting 32, 62
Fire 14
Fireworks 14
Flood, the 72
Forgiveness 45, 54, 68, 73, 107
Friends 4, 32, 45, 70
Frog, Caracole 95

Games 4
Gandhi, Mahatma 24
Giving and taking 82
*Gold 175
Golden Rule 177
Goldilocks 24
Good Samaritan 145

211

Acknowledgments

We are grateful to the following publishers, agents and authors for permission to reprint the copyright material indicated. Every effort has been made to trace the ownership of all copyright material, but in a few cases this has proved impossible. Should any question arise as to the use of any extract, or any error, it is hoped that the publishers will be informed.

Bell and Hyman Ltd. for an extract from *A feather for my cap* by I.O. Eastwick, *A giant's cake* by E.S. Garde, an extract from *Apple Harvest* by Helen Caddy, *Autumn morning* and *Colour* by A. White, *Best of all* by J.M. Westrup, *Dancing on the shore* by M.M. Hutchinson, *Four scarlet berries* by M. Vivian, *I wonder* by Jeannie Kirby, *Lovely things* by H.M. Sarson, *Pudding charms* by Charlotte Druitt Cole, *Tall trees* by Eileen Mathias, all from THE BOOK OF 1000 POEMS.

Blandford Press Ltd. for *A man in space* by D.M. Prescott, *A spike of green* by B. Baker, *Everyday things* by Jean Ayer, an extract from *God's lovely things* by N.B. Turner, *Grey brothers* by A. M. Montgomery, an extract from *Joseph* by Clive Samson, '*Today*' from *A little child's prayer* by John Bannister Tabb, *Who?* by John Morrison, all from POEMS FOR THE SCHOOL ASSEMBLY.

Brandt & Brandt Literary Agents, Inc. for an extract from *Captain Kidd*, from A BOOK OF AMERICANS by Rosemary and Stephen Vincent Benet © 1933 by Rosemary and Stephen Vincent Benet, © renewed 1961 by Rosemary Carr Benet.

Mrs Jenifer Brown for *Yesterday* by Hugh Chesterman, © Jenifer Brown.

Marchette Chute for *My Dog* and *Christmas*, from AROUND AND ABOUT by Marchette Chute, © 1957 E.P. Dutton.

Collins Publishers for *Little Betty Blue* by A.G. Herbertson, from UNDERNEATH A MUSHROOM (Laurel & Gold).

J.M. Dent & Sons Ltd. and Miss D. Collins for *The Christ Child* by G.K. Chesterton, from THE WILD KNIGHT AND OTHER POEMS.

André Deutsch Ltd. for an extract from *Adventures of Isabel*, and for *The people upstairs*, from I WOULDN'T HAVE MISSED IT by Ogden Nash (André Deutsch 1983).

Dobson Books Ltd. for *Boy and fish*, from COLLECTED POEMS AND VERSES FOR CHILDREN by Leonard Clark.

Doubleday & Company, Inc. for *Rain in the night* by Amelia J. Burr, and *Only my opinion* from GOOSE GRASS RHYMES by Monica Shannon, © 1930 by Doubleday & Company, Inc.

Vilma Dubé for *Croptime*, © Vilma Dubé.

Gerald Duckworth & Co. Ltd. for *The vulture* from COMPLETE VERSE by Hilaire Belloc.

East African Publishing House Ltd. for *African lullaby* (*Lullaby for an African baby*) from AFRICAN POETRY FOR SCHOOLS.

Express Newspapers Ltd. for stories adapted from the SUNDAY EXPRESS — *Birthdays* (9 December 1979), *Two men and a violin* (22 March 1981), and *The man who looked like Father Christmas* (date unknown, roadsweeper story).

Miss Alison Fleming for *Who's in?* by Elizabeth Fleming, © Alison Fleming.

Gill and Macmillan Ltd. for an extract from *The brick* by Michel Quoist, from PRAYERS OF LIFE.

Good News Bible for scripture quotations, © American Bible Society 1976, published by the Bible Societies/Collins.

Granada Publishing Ltd. for *As I put out to the open sea* by M.E. Rose, from THE MORNING COCKEREL BOOK OF READINGS.